CAMPAIGN • 220

OPERATION *CRUSADER* 1941

Rommel in Retreat

KEN FORD   ILLUSTRATED BY JOHN WHITE

Series editor Marcus Cowper

First published in 2010 by Osprey Publishing
Midland House, West Way, Botley, Oxford OX2 0PH, UK
44-02 23rd St, Suite 219, Long Island City, NY 11101, USA
E-mail: info@ospreypublishing.com

A CIP catalogue record for this book is available from the British Library.

ISBN: 978 1 84603 500 5

E-book ISBN: 978 1 84908 277 8

Editorial by Ilios Publishing Ltd, Oxford, UK (www.iliospublishing.com)
Page layout by Mark Holt
Index by Fineline Editorial Service
Typeset in Sabon and Myriad Pro
Originated by PPS Grasmere Ltd
Cartography: Bounford.com
Bird's-eye view artworks: The Black Spot
Battlescene illustrations by John White
Originated by United Graphic Pte Ltd.
Printed in China through Worldprint

10 11 12 13 14   10 9 8 7 6 5 4 3 2 1

ACKNOWLEDGEMENTS

I should like to express my gratitude to the trustees of the Imperial War
Museum, the Bundesarchiv and to Steve Hamilton of Western Desert
Battlefield Tours for permission to use the photographs for which they hold
the copyright.

ARTIST'S NOTE

Readers may care to note that the original paintings from which the
colour plates in this book were prepared are available for private sale.
All reproduction copyright whatsoever is retained by the Publishers.
All enquiries should be addressed to:

John White
5107 C Monroe Road
Charlotte
NC 28205
USA

The Publishers regret that they can enter into no correspondence upon
this matter.

THE IMPERIAL WAR MUSEUM COLLECTIONS

Some of the photos in this book come from the Imperial War Museum's
huge collections, which cover all aspects of conflict involving Britain
and the Commonwealth since the start of the twentieth century.
These rich resources are available online to search, browse and buy
at www.iwmcollections.org.uk. In addition to collections online, you can
visit the visitor rooms where you can explore over 8 million photographs,
thousands of hours of moving images, the largest sound archive of its kind
in the world, thousands of diaries and letters written by people in wartime,
and a huge reference library. To make an appointment, call (020) 7416
5320, or e-mail mail@iwm.org.uk.

Imperial War Museum www.iwm.org.uk

THE WOODLAND TRUST

Osprey Publishing are supporting the Woodland Trust, the UK's leading
woodland conservation charity, by funding the dedication of trees.

Key to military symbols

FOR A CATALOGUE OF ALL BOOKS PUBLISHED BY OSPREY MILITARY
AND AVIATION PLEASE CONTACT:

NORTH AMERICA
Osprey Direct, c/o Random House Distribution Center, 400 Hahn
Road, Westminster, MD 21157
E-mail: uscustomerservice@ospreypublishing.com

ALL OTHER REGIONS
Osprey Direct, The Book Service Ltd, Distribution Centre, Colchester
Road, Frating Green, Colchester, Essex, CO7 7DW
E-mail: customerservice@ospreypublishing.com

www.ospreypublishing.com

CONTENTS

April 1941: Rommel's first offensive pushes Wavell's forces back to Egypt and isolates the port of Tobruk

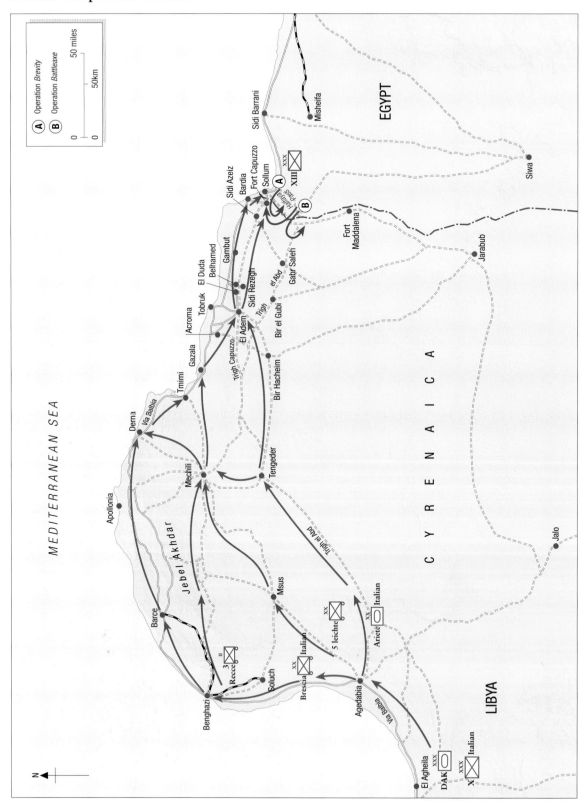

ORIGINS OF THE BATTLE

On 22 June 1941, General Archibald Wavell, Commander-in-Chief Middle East, received a telegram from the British Prime Minister, Winston Churchill, which relieved him of his command. Churchill had been disappointed for some time with the progress being made in North Africa and the Eastern Mediterranean, but it was the recent failure of Operation *Battleaxe* that prompted him to make the move. The Prime Minister had high expectations for the outcome of the operation, believing that the recent reinforcement of British forces in the theatre put Wavell in a strong position to strike hard at the Italians and Germans gathered on the border between Egypt and Libya. He hoped that the blow against Rommel would be decisive and would result in the relief of the besieged port of Tobruk and the elimination of Axis troops from Cyrenaica. When the attack ended in failure just two days after it had begun, Churchill decided that Wavell would have to go.

The move was unfair, for Wavell had actually performed well during his two years as commander-in-chief. His was not an easy command, for in addition to his North African responsibilities Wavell also had to counter Axis moves by the Germans in Greece and Crete as well as those by Vichy French forces in Syria and Iraq. He had begun well and had achieved remarkable successes at the start of the war against the Italians when he conquered almost the whole of Italian East Africa. Under his command, Lieutenant-General O'Connor had pushed back the Italians from the Egyptian border and taken the Cyrenaica province of Libya along with 200,000 prisoners. However, the

A British artillery tractor pulls a limber and gun across the desert ready for the next battle. The crew of the 25-pdr field gun ride on top of their stores and kit on the outside of the Morris C8 4 x 4 Quad. (IWM, E7245)

situation in North Africa deteriorated rapidly when Italian troops in the region were reinforced by the arrival of German units led by Erwin Rommel, the master of armoured warfare. All of O'Connor's gains were soon retaken when Rommel went on the offensive with the Italians and his German 5. leichte-Division and pushed the British back into Egypt. The only gain that Wavell held onto as the Axis tanks sped eastwards was the port of Tobruk. It remained cut off in the rear under a state of complete siege. Its garrison was too weak to achieve a breakout and Rommel could not break in with the forces he had available, although he tried several times.

Wavell twice launched major attacks to relieve Tobruk, but was unable to penetrate the German defences near the border. Each time his effort was too weak and too badly organized to have an impact. The first, Operation *Brevity*, was launched immediately after Rommel's second attempt to capture Tobruk. Wavell had hoped to catch the German commander off balance whilst his supply train was stretched to the limit. It was an ill-planned and premature attack which came to nothing. Wavell then decided to wait for the arrival of a major convoy bringing large numbers of tanks, equipment and reinforcements from England. This 'Tiger' convoy carried amongst other things 53 Hurricane fighters and 295 new tanks. With these Wavell hoped to gain a favourable balance of power with which to strike at the enemy. When the convoy arrived Churchill demanded immediate aggressive action and put pressure on his commander-in-chief to launch a new attack. Wavell insisted that he needed time to effectively build up his strength and train his forces, but Churchill would not countenance any more delays. Operation *Battleaxe*, he demanded, should begin as soon as possible.

Battleaxe was launched as Churchill had insisted and it failed miserably. Within two days Wavell's XIII Corps, under the command of Lieutenant-General Beresford Pierse, was in retreat, scrambling to get back behind the British defences along the border. Rommel had masterminded a sweeping counter-attack immediately after Wavell's armour had pressed forwards, trying to isolate the advance formations of XIII Corps. Wavell's commanders were caught off guard and could do nothing but pull back to prevent a rout. *Battleaxe* was the third successive defeat at the hands of Rommel in six

The winding road that led over Halfaya (Hellfire) Pass, which was for so long the front line between Eighth Army and Axis forces. (IWM, CM2133)

months and the German general was beginning to build an unbeatable reputation amongst those fighting in North Africa on both sides.

The outcome of *Battleaxe* was that Wavell had to go, even though many thought that Churchill's pressure to start the battle prematurely was the cause of the latest failure. A new man now had to be found to head up the Mediterranean theatre, one who was experienced enough at the highest level. General Sir Claude Auchinleck was, to Churchill, the obvious choice. He was a very senior officer who had already seen action in the war when commanding the British part of the failed Anglo-French engagement in Norway in 1940. He was, at that time, Commander-in-Chief India and Churchill now decided that he should take over the Middle East command. Wavell would replace him as Commander-in-Chief India. The swapping of commands would in some ways allow Wavell to continue his army career without there being any hint of demotion.

As soon as Auchinleck arrived at his new headquarters in Egypt he was warned by his boss in London, the Chief of the Imperial General Staff General Sir John Dill, to be prepared for pressure from the British Cabinet advising him to attack in the desert as soon as possible. Very soon this pressure began to be applied when Churchill sent a signal to him asking when he proposed to resume the offensive, urging immediate action. As he settled into his new command Auchinleck came to realize that he was responsible for the conduct of war on two fronts. He knew that before he could concentrate on Rommel and the desert war he had to consolidate British power in Iraq and Syria. He also knew that he could not go on the offensive until he had achieved some sort of superiority in armour over his Axis opponents. He replied to Churchill along those lines, but failed to convince the Prime Minister. The pressure for immediate action against enemy forces in Libya continued right up to the start of Operation *Crusader*.

Churchill had good reasons for insisting that an early offensive was essential to the British war effort. Germany's attack on Russia had made Stalin a new ally for Britain. The common goal of beating the Axis powers meant that Britain had to give some direct support to the Russians. The only possible way of doing this was to force the enemy to fight on two fronts; any troops that could be kept tied down in North Africa were troops that could not be employed against the Red Army on the Russian front. British success in the desert could also induce the French colonies in North Africa away from Vichy and might well influence Spain and Turkey to keep out of the war. It might also encourage the USA to join the conflict.

There were other issues that a resumption of the attack might achieve that were much closer to Auchinleck's command. Progress westwards would not only relieve the besieged garrison in Tobruk and alleviate the need for the Royal Navy to keep it supplied, the advance would also free up airfields in Cyrenaica that the RAF could use to give better coverage to Mediterranean shipping, to attack enemy supply lines and to give some respite to the battered island of Malta.

Auchinleck, however, would not be pressured into acting before he was absolutely ready, for Rommel's forces had been further reinforced and were now much stronger. The 5. leichte-Division had been upgraded to Panzer-Division status with the arrival of a Panzergrenadier regiment and became 21. Panzer-Division. The 15. Panzer-Division had also arrived in North Africa to allow the establishment of the Deutsches Afrika Korps (DAK). Auchinleck decided that the new offensive, codename Operation *Crusader*, would begin on 1 November 1941 and not before. This was over four months after the failure of *Battleaxe*. Churchill remained unimpressed. He was livid that Britain's only land forces in contact with the enemy were sitting it out in the desert and suggested that the commander-in-chief should return to London for consultation. If the Prime Minister thought that Auchinleck could be bullied into attacking earlier he was mistaken. The desert commander stood up to Churchill, sticking to his original decision and refusing to budge on the matter.

Auchinleck returned to Cairo somewhat shaken by the personal pressure that had been applied to him, vowing never again to allow political demands to interfere with purely military decisions. It had been finally agreed in London that *Crusader* would begin on 1 November and that his desert force would be elevated to an army command. Also agreed was the appointment of Lieutenant-General Alan Cunningham to that command, even though Churchill favoured Lieutenant-General Maitland Wilson for the post. The Prime Minister was beginning to regret that Auchinleck had ever been appointed Commander-in-Chief Middle East.

BELOW

The Australian 9th Division had held the fortress of Tobruk ever since Rommel's forces had surrounded the port area in April. In mid-September these troops were relieved by the men of British 70th Division as Maj. Gen. Scobie's formation took over the defence of the isolated garrison. Here, British and Australian troops exchange pleasantries during the changeover. (IWM, E6122)

BELOW RIGHT

A 60-pdr gun, a veteran of World War I, firing from a well-camouflaged position in the desert. These guns were obsolete by the start of World War II and saw action only in medium artillery regiments in France with the British Expeditionary Force, and in the early fighting in North Africa. (IWM, E6513)

CHRONOLOGY

1941

12 February Generalleutnant Erwin Rommel arrives in North Africa with the 5. leichte-Division to help the Italians in their struggle with the British.

23 March Rommel captures El Agheila and begins Italian/German offensive into Cyrenaica, pushing British forces under the command of Gen. Wavell back towards Egypt.

11 April The port of Tobruk is surrounded and placed under a state of siege whilst Rommel's mobile forces advance to the Egyptian border.

11–17 April Rommel attempts to capture Tobruk quickly, but is beaten off with considerable losses.

30 April A major Axis attack is launched against Tobruk assisted by 70 tanks, but once again fails with the loss of over 1,000 men.

15–17 May General Wavell goes back on the offensive with Major-General Gott and his Support Group launching Operation *Brevity*, an attack along the coast reinforced with all available armour. It fails, after some early success, through lack of strength.

15–17 June Wavell's second attack along the coastal region towards Tobruk, Operation *Battleaxe*, again fails after a strong counter-attack by Rommel's Afrika Korps.

22 June General Wavell is replaced as Commander-in-Chief Middle East by Gen. Claude Auchinleck.

July–November Auchinleck builds up his forces ready to launch Operation *Crusader* and refuses to yield to pressure from the Prime Minister to launch his campaign prematurely. Rommel also consolidates his forces ready for a massive attack on Tobruk. British Eighth Army is formed under the command of Lt. Gen. Alan Cunningham.

18 November Eighth Army launches Operation *Crusader* with the armour of XXX Corps attacking towards Gabr Saleh hoping to lure the Afrika Korps into battle.

19 November Rommel refuses to move his armour against XXX Corps believing its advance to be just a diversionary attack to draw his attention away from Tobruk. British XIII Corps moves north-east in an attempt to get behind Axis forces positioned along the frontier. With no sign of the German armour, 7th Armoured Brigade is sent towards Tobruk against negligible resistance and takes the airfield at Sidi Rezegh. The 22nd Armoured Brigade advances to Bir el Gubi where it clashes with the Italian 132ª Divisione Corazzata 'Ariete' and suffers heavy losses.

20 November	The Afrika Korps advances towards Gabr Saleh and meets the lone 4th Armoured Brigade only, not the three British armoured brigades originally planned by Lt. Gen. Cunningham. The British brigade suffers heavy losses in the tank battle that follows. The 7th Armoured Brigade makes progress against the German 90. leichte-Division near Sidi Rezegh.
21 November	After dealing harshly with the British at Gabr Saleh, the Afrika Korps turns north-east and attacks the rear of 7th Armoured Brigade near Sidi Rezegh. Cunningham orders the 70th Division to begin to break out of its encirclement at Tobruk and, after a hard day's fighting, it manages to carve out a corridor through the Axis lines.
22–23 November	Major tank battle takes place between Gabr Saleh and Sidi Rezegh as Eighth Army's three armoured brigades engage the Afrika Korps. The outcome is disastrous for the British, but not fatal as both sides lose a large number of tanks.
24 November	Rommel thinks he has finished off the British armour and makes a dash for the frontier to give some respite to his forces there that are being attacked by British XIII Corps. Cunningham is appalled by this move and contemplates a total withdrawal of Eighth Army.
25 November	Fighting on the frontier is confused, with Rommel's tanks making ineffective piecemeal attacks and suffering from a lack of fuel. Auchinleck urges Cunningham to ignore Rommel's moves and concentrate on attacking the area of Sidi Rezegh.
26 November	The New Zealand Division from XIII Corps advances along the escarpment near Sidi Rezegh to meet up with the Tobruk Garrison. Rommel's absence from the western side of the battlefield allows XXX Corps to build up its tank strength. Cunningham is relieved as commander of Eighth Army and replaced by Major-General Neil Ritchie.
27 November	The British continue to attack in the west and Rommel realizes that a crisis in the battle is taking place near Sidi Rezegh. He orders his armour to return westwards to attack XXX Corps once again.
28–30 November	The battle now hinges on the actions around Sidi Rezegh. Ritchie introduces more and more infantry whilst Rommel struggles to take the initiative with his steadily depleting Panzer force. The New Zealand Division is badly mauled and withdraws to Egypt for a refit, being replaced by the 4th Indian Division.
1–6 December	Fighting is sporadic as Ritchie brings forward fresh troops and Rommel tries to gain a position from which to concentrate his armour against XXX Corps. He tries one last time to drive through to Tobruk on 4 December, but the attack lacks strength and fails.
7 December	It is made clear to Rommel that his forces are growing weaker whilst Eighth Army is growing stronger by moving formations up from Egypt. Rommel orders a fighting withdrawal back to the Gazala line.
10 December	After a siege of eight months, Tobruk is liberated. Eighth Army gradually moves westwards behind the retreating Axis troops.
15 December	The attack on the Gazala Line begins with a frontal assault followed by a flanking move through the southern desert by 4th Armoured Brigade, which forces Rommel into a full retreat across Cyrenaica and into Tripolitania.

28–30 December The Afrika Korps turns and confronts 2nd Armoured Brigade near Mersa Brega, forcing a sharp action which halts the chase by Eighth Army. Both sides are now exhausted.

1942

1 January Rommel orders a final retreat into the prepared positions at El Agheila, the point from which he launched his first offensive against the British nine months earlier.

ABOVE LEFT
A 6in. field gun firing from its camouflaged position near the frontier. The gun, a veteran of World War I, saw limited service in the theatre, but by the time of the *Crusader* battle it was obsolete. (IWM, E7687)

ABOVE RIGHT
A brigade signals office in the field. This well turned-out team of signallers have obviously smartened themselves up for the cameraman and give an impression of total control and organization. In the heat of battle things were less calm. (IWM, 6261)

LEFT
South African sappers unearth German 'Teller' anti-tank mines and bring them to an assembly point where they will be defused and made safe. (IWM, E7601)

OPPOSING COMMANDERS

When the British finally launched their new offensive, Operation *Crusader*, after four months of waiting, they did so with an entirely fresh set of commanders: the commander-in-chief of the theatre was new, the army commander was new and both of the corps commanders were new. None of them had experience of action in the desert and none had fought with armoured formations before. In contrast, facing Eighth Army across the border in Libya was an Axis force led by one of the greatest proponents of armoured warfare of that time, with subordinate commanders who had not only fought in a number of tank battles, but were also acclimatized to fighting in the desert.

BRITISH COMMANDERS

Major-General Frank Messervy (right), Commander 4th Indian Division, in conversation with one of his staff officers. (IWM, E7235)

General Sir Claude Auchinleck (1884–1981) was a soldier of the Indian Army. There were marked differences between the British and the Indian Armies; they were, in the words of a recent historian 'two professional worlds separated by mutual pride'. Both groups were entirely different and each saw the other as being inferior. Being from the colonialist Indian Army was a slight handicap for Auchinleck, for he was away from the power base of military politics in England and knew very few of the senior officers that he was about to command. His long service in India also left him with little knowledge of armoured warfare. He did, nonetheless, bring with him a big personal reputation, for 'the Auk' as he was affectionately called, was well known throughout both armies as an especially gifted and brave commander.

Auchinleck was a modest and somewhat austere man who shied away from publicity. His unpretentious style set him close to the soldiers under his command. Most of his army life was spent far away from his homeland. During World War I he served in Egypt, Aden and Mesopotamia. Between the wars he held various posts in India including time as an instructor at the Staff College at Quetta. He was recognized as being an exceptional officer and gradually rose to command the 3rd Indian Division in 1939. In 1940 he was

General Auchinleck (left) in conversation with the commander of the 7th Support Group, Brig. 'Jock' Campbell. (IWM, E8260)

called back to England first to command IV Corps and then the Anglo-French invasion of Norway. The expedition to Norway was a failure, but none of the blame rested with Auchinleck. His rise in status continued for he was given command of V Corps in June 1940 and then, soon after, an army command when he took over as head of Southern Command. By this time political events in the Far East were deteriorating, with Japan threatening the stability of the region. Auchinleck was promoted to the rank of full general and sent back to his beloved India to assume the position of commander-in-chief.

When he took over in the Middle East he was faced with a daunting prospect, for besides having responsibility for Britain's only forces in contact with the enemy, Auchinleck was also accountable for quelling the unrest in Palestine and Iraq as well as for action against the Vichy French in Syria. British forces were, however, in the process of being reorganized as more reinforcements were gradually being received into the theatre. It would now be possible to raise a second corps in Egypt to join XIII Corps, thus making an army command. This was designated Eighth Army and a further army, Ninth Army, was being raised to deal with the Iraq/Syria problem. Lieutenant-General Maitland Wilson was given Ninth Army, whilst Lt. Gen. Sir Alan Cunningham was raised to the head of Eighth Army.

Lieutenant-General Sir Alan Cunningham (1887–1983) had served with the Royal Artillery in World War I, where he won the Military Cross and the Distinguished Service Order. He rose through various commands during the inter-war years eventually commanding the 5th Anti-Aircraft Division at the outbreak of World War II. In the early war years he was progressively GOC (General Officer Commanding) to the 66th, 9th and 51st Divisions, training the formations ready for action. In late 1940 he was promoted to lieutenant-general and given command of British East African Forces in Kenya. It was here that he enhanced his reputation. General Wavell ordered Cunningham to advance into Italian Somaliland to engage Mussolini's forces there. This he did with resounding success and then invaded Italian-held Abyssinia (modern

Lieutenant-General Alan Cunningham, Commander British Eighth Army. Cunningham took over the newly designated army at the end of August 1941, three months before the start of the *Crusader* offensive. (IWM, E6661)

Ethiopia). Cunningham advanced over 1,600km with a small force to Addis Ababa and defeated the Italian Army under the Duke of Aosta, clearing Italian possession completely from East Africa. Over 50,000 Italians were captured for the loss of only 500 of Cunningham's force.

Cunningham's victory in Abyssinia earmarked him for further operational command, so that when the new Eighth Army was raised Auchinleck saw him as the perfect man to lead it into battle. The eastern Mediterranean was becoming something of a family affair, for the naval Commander-in-Chief Mediterranean was his elder brother **Admiral Andrew Browne Cunningham (1883–1963)**. Admiral Cunningham had a formidable reputation in the Mediterranean gained through his bold actions against the Italian Fleet at Taranto and Cape Matapan, and by his timely evacuation of British and Commonwealth forces from Crete in 1941. He had blunted Mussolini's surface naval power in the Mediterranean and could therefore, for the most part, concentrate on keeping Auchinleck's forces well supplied and the island of Malta free. Supporting both the Royal Navy and Auchinleck's ground forces was the Western Desert Air Force led by **Air Vice-Marshal Arthur Coningham (1895–1948)**.

Like Auchinleck, Lt. Gen. Alan Cunningham ascended to the desert command through his reputation, but without the necessary experience in handling tank formations. He was a gunner, with virtually no understanding of armoured warfare – this was also true of all British officers of his rank. He had arrived onto a battleground that was dominated by the forces of Rommel, one of the most famous proponents of mobile warfare. Cunningham needed all the help he could get to ensure that British armour was used effectively. Unfortunately, his subordinate commanders were also a little short of experience of using armour in battle.

Lieutenant-General Charles Willoughby Norrie (1893–1977) commanded XXX Corps, which contained the bulk of the British armour. Although a cavalry officer, he was not the first choice for this command. The corps had originally been given to Lieutenant-General Vyvyan Pope, a tank officer with long experience in various armoured formations. Unfortunately, Pope was

BELOW
Lieutenant-General Charles Willoughby Norrie, Commander British XXX Corps, makes radio contact with one of his forward divisions during the battle. (IWM, E7150)

BELOW RIGHT
Major-General William 'Strafer' Gott, Commander 7th Armoured Division. Gott's nickname was a pun on the German phrase *Gott strafe England* (God punishes England). Gott later commanded XIII Corps during the Gazala battle and was then promoted to the command of Eighth Army in August 1942, but was killed in an air crash on the way to take up his appointment. (IWM, E7515)

killed with some of his staff in an air crash just six weeks before the start of Operation *Crusader*. Norrie stepped in at the last minute when preparations for the attack were well underway. He had previously commanded 1st Armoured Brigade and 2nd Armoured Division before joining 1st Armoured Division in England. He had not seen armoured action with any of these formations.

Lieutenant-General Alfred Godwin-Austen (1889–1963) who commanded Eighth Army's veteran infantry formation, XIII Corps, was also a new appointee. He was an infantryman and had seen service in World War I. Like Gen. Cunningham he came to the theatre from East Africa. His 12th African Division formed part of Cunningham's East African Force and his formation took part in the defeat of the Italians in Abyssinia. Before then he had commanded 8th Division in Palestine.

AXIS COMMANDERS

In contrast to the number of changes in command that had been made in the British forces, the Axis senior commanders remained static. The one change prior to *Crusader* that had been implemented was at the top. The Axis forces fighting the British in North Africa were all part of the command of **Generale d'Armata Ettore Bastico (1876–1972)** as Commander-in-Chief Libya. He had arrived in the theatre on 19 July from his previous role as Governor-General of the Dodecanese Islands. Bastico had earlier commanded the 1ª Divisione Camicie Nere '23 Marzo' in Abyssinia in 1936 and the Corpo Truppe Volontarie in Spain fighting for the Nationalists under General Franco. Bastico reported directly to **Maresciallo Ugo Cavallero (1880–1943)**, the *commando supremo* in Rome.

Bastico's position made him overall leader of all Italian and German troops in North Africa, including Rommel and his staff. In reality, his influence was mainly over the Italians and in the implementation of the strategy set by Rome regarding Italian ambitions in the region. He had three corps commanders in the theatre: **Generale di Corpo d'Armata Gastone Gambara (1890–1962)** led XX Corpo d'Armata, **Generale di Corpo d'Armata Enea Navarrini** was at the head of XXI Corpo and **Generale di**

Corpo d'Armata Benvenuto Gioda commanded X Corpo. All of these corps commanders had seen action in North Africa and elsewhere. Gambara had led a corps in the Spanish Civil War and in Greece, Navarrini had been a divisional commander in Greece and Gioda had previously commanded the 4ª Divisione Camicie Nere '3 Gennaio' in France.

The German contribution to the North African campaign in mid-1941 still mainly consisted of the Afrika Korps and some Luftwaffe troops. Since arriving in the theatre in an advisory and supporting role, German numbers and influence had increased to the point that they were organizing and carrying out much of the fighting. At the head of this German contribution was the Luftwaffe field marshal, **Generalfeldmarschall Albert Kesselring (1885–1960)**. Kesselring was Commander-in-Chief Mediterranean at the head of all German forces and was Rommel's immediate superior. He formed the link between the Italian High Command and Berlin and undertook to integrate Italian strategy with that of the German High Command (Oberkommando der Wehrmacht, or OKW) and with Rommel's intentions in the desert. His

General der Panzertruppe Erwin Rommel, Commander Panzergruppe Afrika, had by the start of Operation *Crusader* built up a formidable reputation as a practitioner of armoured warfare. The desert was the ideal place in which to demonstrate his talents and his early successes brought him great fame. (US National Archives)

amiable personality and good relations with the Italians helped to ease tensions and soften the often-stormy relationship that existed between Rommel and his Italian allies.

By the middle of 1941 the commander of the Afrika Korps, **General der Panzertruppe Erwin Rommel (1891–1944)**, had achieved a legendary status amongst those fighting in North Africa on both sides. His application of armoured tactics in the wide open spaces of the desert was masterly. Since arriving in the theatre he had driven the British back 640km to the Egyptian border and had repulsed two armoured operations against his forces. He had isolated the large port of Tobruk and now stood poised to overwhelm its garrison and continue the advance to the river Nile.

Rommel was a successful general and the old axiom that 'success breeds success' was, in his case, very true. It had been so throughout his army career. He was a well-decorated commander during World War I, winning Germany's highest award for bravery, the Pour le Mérite Cross. During the inter-war years he penned a successful book on infantry tactics, commanded the War School at Wiener-Neustadt and became head of Hitler's security battalion in Poland. This last appointment brought him into close contact with the Führer and raised his profile amongst the leaders of the OKW. His exploits at the head of the 7. Panzer-Division during the battle of France in 1940 sealed his reputation as a bold and energetic commander of armour. When the call went out for an experienced general to advise and support the Italians in North Africa, Rommel was the obvious choice.

Generalleutnant Ludwig Crüwell (1892–1958) led the Afrika Korps during the *Crusader* battle. He had taken over command of the formation on 15 August 1941 after Rommel had assumed command of the newly raised Panzergruppe Afrika. Prior to this, Crüwell had led the 11. Panzer-Division on the Eastern Front. He had served in the cavalry throughout World War I and was an early recruit to the Panzer arm of the Wehrmacht during the inter-war years. During the *Crusader* battles, Crüwell's capable handling of the Afrika Korps brought him much credit and led to his promotion in December 1941 to *General der Panzertruppe*.

Crüwell's Panzer corps comprised two Panzer divisions and the Afrika Infantry Division (Division Afrika zur besondern verfügung, or Div zbv Afrika). Both of the armoured divisions were commanded by generals experienced in tank warfare. **Generalleutnant Johann von Ravenstein (1889–1962)** had moved to North Africa in May to replace Generalmajor Johannes Streich at the head of 5. leichte-Division. Streich had been relieved of his command during the attack on Tobruk after he had challenged Rommel's judgement. Ravenstein had, like Rommel, served in World War I and had been awarded the Pour le Mérite Cross for bravery during the battle of the Marne. He arrived to command the 5. leichte-Division at a time when the division was being enlarged, strengthened and redesignated as the 21 Panzer-Division. The other armoured formation in the Africa Korps was the 15. Panzer-Division, commanded by **Generalleutnant Walther Neumann-Silkow (1891–1941)**, a veteran of the campaign in France in 1940. He had also served for a time as acting commander of 8. Panzer-Division during the attacks on Yugoslavia and Russia shortly before joining Rommel in Africa. The Afrika Division was later to be known as the 90. leichte-Division and at the time of Operatio *Crusader* was commanded by **Generalmajor Max Sümmermann.**

OPPOSING ARMIES

Auchinleck was resolute in his decision that he would not open an offensive until his forces were completely ready and had to withstand much pressure from his political masters in London to hold on to that conviction. The time between the failure of *Battleaxe* and the start of *Crusader* was used to make this possible. Rommel was under less pressure, for the OKW and the Italian High Command were content for him to hold onto the frontier in strength and to be prepared for the British onslaught when it came.

BRITISH FORCES

Since the failure of Operation *Battleaxe* more tanks had been arriving from England, both as replacements for losses and as reinforcements with formations new to the theatre. Auchinleck felt that to be ready to launch Operation *Crusader* he needed a 3:2 ratio of superiority in tank strength over the enemy. This would involve assembling the equivalent of at least two armoured divisions and a suitable number of infantry formations. This, however, was not to be. The 1st Armoured Division, earmarked to join Eighth Army, would not wholly arrive in Egypt until early in 1942, but its 22nd Armoured Brigade did arrive on 4 October and was immediately assigned to 7th Armoured Division for the forthcoming battle. Its tanks were the newer

Crews of two British Stuart tanks are briefed before an operation. Tank crews were generally happy with this newly arrived American light tank despite its short range. They were impressed with its high speed and mechanical reliability, in stark contrast to the poor performance of the British cruisers. (IWM, 6288)

version of the Crusader cruiser tank, armed, as were all British tanks in the theatre, with a 2-pdr gun. The tank was relatively fast and manoeuvrable, but was mechanically unreliable and lacked a gun that could compete with the newer Panzers. Eighth Army still had many older cruiser tanks in its command from earlier times, such as the Cruiser A13.

Also being shipped into the theatre in large numbers was the American Stuart tank, sometimes called the Honey. This was a light tank armed with a 37mm gun, the performance of which virtually matched the 2-pdr gun. The tank was small, lightly armoured and designed as a reconnaissance tank, but with Eighth Army during Operation *Crusader* it was employed as a cruiser tank. The tank was fast and manoeuvrable, but had a limited range and required frequent refuelling.

Supporting the infantry were two army tank brigades each containing two types of infantry-support tank. Both of these were armed with 2-pdr guns: the obsolete pre-war Matilda was slow but heavily armoured and was gradually being replaced by another vehicle labelled as an infantry tank, but actually designed as a cruiser, the Valentine.

The main strike arm of Eighth Army was the 7th Armoured Division. This formation nominally contained two armoured brigades, the 7th and the 4th Armoured Brigades, each of which contained three tank battalions. For Operation *Crusader* the division was supplemented with the 22nd Armoured Brigade and its three tank battalions. This gave Cunningham nine tank battalions in his main armoured force as opposed to the four German tank battalions in the two Panzer divisions of the Afrika Korps and three in the Italian 132[a] Divisione Corazzata 'Ariete'. These figures excluded light reconnaissance tanks. The 7th Armoured Division also contained the 7th Support Group, a motorized brigade of artillery and infantry. At the start of the campaign Eighth Army had a total of 477 tanks: 32 early cruisers, 62 cruisers (A13), 210 Crusaders and 173 Stuarts. In Tobruk the 32nd Army Tank Brigade had 32 cruisers, 25 Stuarts and 69 Matildas, and supporting XIII Corps on the frontier was 1st Army Tank Brigade containing three cruisers and 132 infantry tanks of which roughly half were Matildas and half Valentines.

Crucial to the control of the battlefield was the anti-tank gun. Unfortunately for the British, their main anti-tank weapon was the ubiquitous

Two Crusader cruiser tanks move forwards during the operation. This picture was taken on 26 November at the height of the tank battles around Sidi Rezegh. The Crusader's main 2-pdr weapon seems tiny in comparison with those found on German tanks. (IWM, E6724)

The men of a British Bren-gun position keep watch from within their stone sangar. These defensive posts were constructed by collecting together boulders and pieces of rock to form some sort of protection from enemy fire. The ground was often too hard to dig more conventional refuges. (IWM, 6379)

2-pdr. At ranges in excess of 1,000m it was practically useless. To do any appreciable damage to enemy armour it had to engage at ranges shorter than this, which of course exposed its crews to great danger. The British did have their 25-pdr field artillery pieces in large numbers and these could be used against tanks when firing solid shot, but the gun/howitzer was not primarily an anti-tank weapon.

For Operation *Crusader*, Cunningham planned to use two corps in the attack: XXX Corps, commanded by Lt. Gen. Norrie, and XIII Corps, commanded by Lt. Gen. Godwin-Austen. Norrie's XXX Corps contained 7th Armoured Division, 1st South African Division and 22nd Guards Brigade. Godwin-Austen's XIII Corps consisted of the 4th Indian Division, 2nd New Zealand Division and the 1st Army Tank Brigade. The besieged garrison in Tobruk was also expected to play a role in the forthcoming battle. The 70th Division supplemented by the Polish 1st Carpathian Brigade and the 32nd Army Tank Brigade would join in the *Crusader* offensive when the opportune moment arrived for them to break out of the Axis perimeter that surrounded the fortress area. The 2nd South African Division remained in Egypt as army reserve.

Along with the build-up of ground forces, the RAF in Egypt had been growing in strength ready for the offensive. What had originally been just 204 Group had now become the Western Desert Air Force under the command of Air Vice-Marshal Arthur Coningham. This was a large, flexible force containing 16 squadrons of fighters, bombers and tactical reconnaissance aircraft. Replacement and maintenance organzations had been overhauled to keep the squadrons well supplied with new and repaired aircraft during the forthcoming campaign. Lessons learned from Operation *Battleaxe* led to the formation of a joint Air Support Control at each corps headquarters so that aircraft could be quickly directed on to targets reported by the troops. At the start of the battle the RAF had 650 aircraft in North Africa of which 550 were serviceable. More support could be given by the 74 aircraft, 66 of them serviceable, which were based in Malta. This gave the Desert Air Force numerical superiority over the enemy, who had 342 serviceable aircraft out of a total of 536.

These were the main forces that Eighth Army planned to launch against the enemy. Auchinleck knew that he could not wait for the perfect moment to attack for pressure from London required that the offensive should be launched before the enemy could overrun the Tobruk fortress. He had to go with the forces already in the theatre.

AXIS FORCES

After the defeat of Operation *Battleaxe*, Rommel's place within the Axis hierarchy was assured. His continuing domination of the British strengthened his position as the actual operational commander of Axis forces in Cyrenaica. During *Battleaxe* he had commanded only the Afrika Korps, albeit with some influence over a few of the Italian divisions, but most of the tactical decisions were down to him. It was becoming clear that he was now the man to take total control over all Axis forces engaged with the British. On 1 July Rommel was promoted to *General der Panzertruppe* and, on 15 August, his command was elevated to Panzergruppe Afrika.

The changes did not mean that the Italian senior commanders were now to be subservient to Rommel; they still had actual command of the theatre. Generale Bastico was Commander-in-Chief Libya and insisted on retaining the Italian XX Corpo d'Armata under his control even though it was part of Panzergruppe Afrika, and, on paper at least, Rommel was subordinate to him. The Italian XXI Corpo also joined Rommel's new command, although the formation was not formally assigned to Rommel for Bastico still wanted everyone to know that it was he who was running the campaign in North Africa. So Rommel had two Italian corps in his Panzergruppe Afrika, one of which he could use as he directed and the other he had to ask permission for before he could deploy the formation.

These moves now placed three corps comprising ten divisions effectively in Rommel's hands: the Deutsches Afrika Korps, commanded by Gen.Lt. Crüwell, with 15. Panzer-Division, 21. Panzer-Division, the Afrika Infantry

A captured Panzerspähwagen SdKfz 231 eight-wheel armoured car is loaded onto a tank conveyor, just after the start of the *Crusader* battle. These heavy reconnaissance vehicles, armed with a 20mm cannon, were held in a position of awe by the crews of their British counterparts in view of their size and power. IWM, 6710)

Division (90. leichte-Division) and the Italian 55ª Divisione 'Savona'; Italian XX Corpo d'Armata, commanded by Generale Gastone Gambara, with the 132ª Divisione Corazzata 'Ariete' and the 101ª Divisione Motorizzate 'Trieste' and the Italian XXI Corpo, commanded by Generale Enea Navarrini, with the 17ª Divisione 'Pavia', 25ª Divisione 'Bologna' and 27ª Divisione 'Brescia' infantry divisions, together with the 102ª Divisione 'Trento'.

The Italian 55ª Divisione 'Savona', which had been placed in the Afrika Korps, contained three infantry regiments whereas each of the other Italian infantry divisions in XXI Corpo all had just two regiments of infantry. The 102ª Divisione 'Trento' had two motorized infantry regiments and a motorized regiment of *bersaglieri*, although the division can be seen as being motorized in name only for it was 80 per cent deficient in transport. Each of these regiments comprised two battalions.

The Panzer divisions in Gen.Lt. Crüwell's Afrika Korps both had one Panzer regiment and one rifle regiment and both had a reconnaissance battalion of armoured cars. The Afrika Division was a curious formation that was later to be renamed the 90. leichte-Division during the battle. It had been formed from various independent units that were already in North Africa, with the addition of further troops that arrived in August 1941 by air. One of its two regiments, Infanterie-Regiment 361, consisted mostly of German members of the Foreign Legion who had been coerced into joining the Wehrmacht in France in the first days of the Vichy government. Their experience of the desert made them a valuable addition to Crüwell's corps.

With the enlargement of his command to *Panzergruppe* status, Rommel was provided with an enlarged headquarters. A complete new staff to man this new headquarters was shipped to him from Germany under the command of Generalmajor Alfred Gause. It was the German practice to train and produce staffs as self-sufficient units, with the group working as a team, able to understand each other's roles and responsibilities and to run a battlefield headquarters from scratch. With Gause behind him as his chief of staff, Rommel was able now to concentrate on the important task of countering the British, leaving his administration and supply responsibilities to the experts. Gause served Rommel well in the desert and remained chief of staff in North Africa, even after Rommel had left the theatre, right to the end of May 1943.

A German armoured car beside a knocked-out German tank. The tank is a Panzer III Ausf. G, which belonged to the signals officer of Panzer-Regiment 5 of the 21. Panzer-Division. (IWM, E7061)

At the start of Operation *Crusader* seven tank battalions were available to Rommel, each comprising a number of different types. The two Panzer divisions combined had 70 Panzer IIs, 139 Panzer IIIs and 35 of the newer Panzer IVs. The 132^a Divisione Corazzata 'Ariete' had 146 Italian M13/40 tanks. This gave Rommel a total of 390 operational tanks as opposed to Auchinleck's combined strength of 477.

Rommel did, however, have a great advantage in anti-tank weapons. The German main gun was the 50mm Pak 38 and this was used to great effect against British tanks. Almost all of the available Pak 38s were kept within the Afrika Korps, as were the few 88mm guns that had arrived in North Africa. The 88mm was designed as an anti-aircraft weapon, but its formidable power was used against tanks in the desert with devastating effect. The Germans also had some older 37mm anti-tank guns available and a great number of Italian 47mm anti-tank weapons.

The Italian 132^a Divisione Corazzata 'Ariete' on the move. Led by a staff car full of officers, a line of M13/40 tanks advance along a desert track towards the front. (Ufficio Storico Esercito Rome)

ORDERS OF BATTLE

BRITISH FORCES
Commander-in-Chief Middle East – Gen. Sir Claude Auchinleck

EIGHTH ARMY
Lt. Gen. Sir A. Cunningham (until 26 November)
Lt. Gen. N. Ritchie (from 26 November)

Army Troops
2nd South African Division – Maj. Gen. I. de Villiers
   3rd South African Brigade – Brig. C. Borain

4th South African Brigade – Brig. A. Hayton
6th South African Brigade – Brig. F. Cooper

Tobruk Garrison
70th Division – Maj. Gen. R. Scobie
   32nd Army Tank Brigade – Brig. A. Willison
   14th Brigade – Brig. B. Chappel
   16th Brigade – Brig. C. Lomax
   23rd Brigade – Brig. C. Cox
   1st Polish Carpathian Brigade – Col. S. Kopański

Matruh Garrison

2nd South African Brigade – Brig. W. Poole

XIII Corps – Lt. Gen. A. Godwin-Austen

4th Indian Division – Maj. Gen. F. Messervy
   5th Indian Brigade – Brig. D. Russell
   7th Indian Brigade – Brig. H. Briggs
   11th Indian Brigade – Brig. A. Anderson

2nd New Zealand Division – Maj. Gen. B. Freyberg
   4th New Zealand Brigade – Brig. L. Inglis
   5th New Zealand Brigade – Brig. J. Hargest
   6th New Zealand Brigade – Brig. H. Barrowclough

1st Army Tank Brigade – Brig H. Watkins

XXX Corps – Lt. Gen. C. Norrie

7th Armoured Division – Maj. Gen. W. Gott
   4th Armoured Brigade Group – Brig. A. Gatehouse
   7th Armoured Brigade – Brig. G. Davy
   22nd Armoured Brigade – Brig. J. Scott-Cockburn
   7th Support Group – Brig. J. Campbell

1st South African Division – Maj. Gen. G. Brink
   1st South African Brigade – Brig. D. Pienaar
   5th South African Brigade – Brig. B. Armstrong

22nd Guards Brigade – Brig. J. Marriott

AXIS FORCES

Commander-in-Chief North Africa – Generale d'Armata
Ettore Bastico

PANZERGRUPPE AFRIKA

General der Panzertruppe E. Rommel

Deutsches Afrika Korps (DAK) – Gen.Lt. L. Crüwell

15. Panzer-Division – Gen.Lt. W. Neumann-Silkow until
9 December, then Gen.Maj. G. von Vaerst
   Panzer-Regiment 8 – Obstlt. H. Cramer
   Schützen-Regiment 115 – Obst. E. Menny

21. Panzer-Division – Gen.Lt. J. von Ravenstein until
29 November, then Gen.Maj. K. Böttcher from 1 December
   Panzer-Regiment 5 – Obstlt. Stephan (KIA 25 November)
   Schützen-Regiment 104 – Obstlt. G. Knabe

Division zbV Afrika (later 90. leichte-Division) – Gen.Maj.
M. Sümmermann until 10 December, then Gen.Lt. R. Veith
   leichte-Infanterie-Regiment 155 – Obst. Marks
   Afrika-Regiment 361 – Obst. H. von Barby
   Sonderveband (Panzergrenadier) 288 – Obst. Menton

Italian 55ª Divisione 'Savona' – Gen. di Div. F. de Giorgis
   15° Reggimento Fanteria
   16° Reggimento Fanteria
   12° Reggimento Artiglieria

Italian XX Corpo d'Armata – Gen. di Corpo d'Armata G. Gambara

132ª Divisione Corazzata 'Ariete' – Gen. di Div. M. Balotta
   132° Reggimento Carri
   8° Reggimento Bersaglieri Motorizzato
   132° Regimento Artiglieria

101ª Divisione Motorizzate 'Trieste' – Gen. di Div. A. Piazzoni
   65° Reggimento Fanteria Motorizzata
   66° Reggimento Fanteria Motorizzata
   21° Reggimento Artiglieria Motorizzato

Italian XXI Corpo – Gen. di Corpo d'Armata E. Navarrini

17ª Divisione 'Pavia' – Gen. di Div. A. Franceschini
   27° Reggimento di Fanteria
   28° Reggimento di Fanteria
   26° Reggimento di Artiglieria

25ª Divisione 'Bologna' – Gen. di Div. A. Gloria
   39° Reggimento di Fanteria
   40° Reggimento di Fanteria
   205° Reggimento di Artiglieria

27ª Divisione 'Brescia' – Gen. di Div. B. Zambon
   19° Reggimento di Fanteria
   20° Reggimento di Fanteria
   55° Reggimento di Artiglieria

102ª Divisione 'Trento' – Gen. di Div. Stampioni
   61° Reggimento Fanteria Motorizzata
   62° Reggimento Fanteria Motorizzata
   7° Reggimento Bersaglieri Motorizzato
   46° Reggimento Artiglieria Motorizzato

Artillerie Gruppe Böttcher – Gen.Maj. K. Böttcher until 1
December, then Obst. Mickl, whereupon the unit became
Artillerie Gruppe Mickl

OPPOSING PLANS

After the failure of Operation *Battleaxe* it became just a matter of time before a new British offensive was launched. The previous action had shown Auchinleck that good preparation was needed before a new offensive could be mounted. Rommel was in much the same position at the end of *Battleaxe*. He needed reinforcements and supplies with which to build up his command before attacking into Egypt. He also had the beleaguered British outpost of Tobruk in his rear, and the problem of reducing its fortress area and opening up the port to Axis shipping dominated his thinking.

BRITISH PLANS

When, in early October 1942, Auchinleck discussed his forthcoming strategy with the commander of Eighth Army, he proposed two possible courses of action. The first was an ambitious drive across the southern desert to cut Axis communications and supply lines south of Benghazi. Cunningham was not at all comfortable with such a bold move, feeling that his army might well

Before the battle the railway that linked the front to the Egyptian port of Alexandria was extended across the desert to Misheifa. Begun in September, two companies of New Zealand railway troops laid 3km of track each day to complete the task by 15 November. The new railhead at Misheifa allowed supply dumps to be created much closer to the front line so that huge stocks of ammunition, fuel and water could be brought forwards and stockpiled ready to support the Eighth Army in the forthcoming battle. (IWM, E6516)

Disposition of forces just before the *Crusader* battle

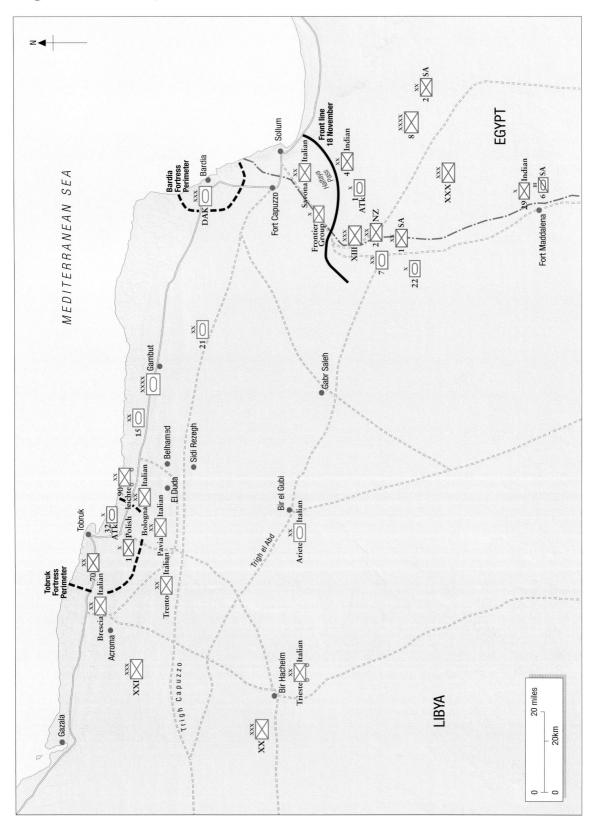

become confounded by supply problems if he moved so far from his sources in Egypt and was also loath to disperse his armoured forces over such a wide area. The proposal was probably a little too bold for the British at that time, which was just as well, for Rommel would have no doubt taken great advantage of the strung-out nature of the British forces and the long exposed flank to the south of his main positions.

The second proposal was more conventional, suggesting a powerful drive towards Tobruk supported by diversionary attacks to induce the belief that a major attack was expected further south. Rommel would then have to decide whether to risk the siege being raised or taking on what would by then be superior tank forces. The major part of the British armour would bring the Afrika Korps to battle and hopefully defeat it. This latter proposition was more acceptable to Cunningham and he agreed with Auchinleck that this should be the basis for further planning. It was also a proposal that was accepted by the theatre's naval and air commanders-in-chief.

Lieutenant-General Cunningham's eventual plan proposed that Eighth Army would advance with XXX Corps on the left to the area of Gabr Saleh, a point in the desert midway between the front line and Bir el Gubi. The move would, it was hoped, induce Rommel to counter XXX Corps with his armour and bring about a decisive showdown where superior numbers of British tanks would defeat the German armour. Once the advance had started, XIII Corps would cross the frontier and swing northwards to get behind those enemy forces holding the front line. These formations would either be completely cut off or forced to withdraw westwards pursued by XIII Corps. The Tobruk garrison would at this point sally out to meet the retreating enemy and join up with the rest of Eighth Army.

Generalfeldmarschall Kesselring (left) talks with Rommel at the end of a meeting of senior Axis commanders. The briefing of German and Italian commanders was to outline Rommel's plans for the seizure of the Tobruk garrison. (Western Desert Battlefield Tours)

RAF salvage crews take a break from the task of hauling back damaged Hurricane fighters to their workshops in the rear. It was important that everything possible was salvaged from the fighters in order to keep other aircraft flying. (IWM, CM 2232)

For the operation XXX Corps would have 7th Armoured Division, 22nd Guards Brigade and the 1st South African Division under command. Auchinleck had insisted that Cunningham place all of his cruiser tanks in XXX Corps to keep the armour concentrated. This left XIII Corps light on armour with only the slow infantry tanks of the 1st Army Tank Brigade under command. Cunningham and the commander of XIII Corps, Lt. Gen. Godwin-Austen, thought that this could lead to problems if Rommel chose to ignore the advance of XXX Corps and turn the tanks of the Afrika Korps against the British infantry attacks along the frontier. Without cruiser tanks to counter this move, XIII Corps would have only its artillery and the ineffective 2-pdr anti-tank gun to use against them, neither of which were capable of staving off a massed Panzer attack.

Auchinleck would not be moved on his decision; he was adamant that the most effective British armour should be concentrated in XXX Corps to deal with the Afrika Korps. As a compromise, he suggested that Lt. Gen. Norrie's XXX Corps should also be made responsible for XIII Corps' left flank as it advanced. Not surprisingly Norrie objected to this decision. He argued that the order to protect XIII Corps' flank would mean that he might be forced to split his armour to do so. He also felt that if Rommel did not take the bait and move with his Panzers to meet him at Gabr Saleh, he would like to advance further towards Tobruk around the Sidi Resegh–El Adem area to bring about this confrontation. If he did this, part of his tank force would have to be left to protect XIII Corps. His objections were noted, but Auchinleck's decision

stood. It was felt that the concentration of armour at Gabr Saleh would enable it to be moved in any direction to meet with whichever threat developed. This decision seemed to be the correct one when news arrived that the Italian 132[a] Divisione Corazzata 'Ariete' had moved to the area of Bir el Gubi, 48km across open desert from the proposed British concentration point at Gabr Saleh, and posed a new threat from the south-west.

The diversionary part of the operation was to be an advance towards Jalo far out in the southern desert by Oasis Group, made up of the 29th Independent Infantry Brigade Group and the 6th South African Armoured Car Regiment. The moves were designed to distract Rommel's attention from the main operation by creating movement between Jalo and Jarabub. The force would then seize an airfield from which the RAF would bomb the coastal region near Benghazi to give the impression that a major attack was to be launched at the rear of Panzerarmee Afrika from the south. Before the operation dummy supply dumps, lorries and tanks were assembled and there was a great increase in signal traffic to simulate the gathering of a great force on the southern frontier. The Long Range Desert Group was also active in the south and in the rear of the coastal strip, monitoring Axis traffic along the main roads and taking every opportunity to harass the enemy as circumstances permitted. Despite all of this effort, Rommel was not influenced by these moves, and the diversionary advance across the southern desert was plagued with supply difficulties and did not influence the conduct of the battle.

To keep Eighth Army in the field, fighting a battle that would inevitably stretch far away from its sources of supply, a great amount of administrative work was required. The build-up for the offensive began back in the summer with an extension of the railway from the great supply port of Alexandria to a new railhead at Misheifa along with a lengthening of the water pipeline from Matruh. Huge stocks of ammunition, fuel and water were brought forwards and new supply dumps set up near the frontier, ready to support Eighth Army's attack. From the railhead three forward bases were organized, each stocked with one week of supplies which amounted to over 32,000 tons: one in the south for Oasis Group, one at Thalata for XXX Corps and one near the coast at Sidi Barrani for XIII Corps. From these, much closer to the front, six forward Field Maintenance Centres were established to ship the supplies forwards to the fighting troops.

AXIS PLANS

In the autumn of 1941, Rommel knew that he was facing the threat of a new British offensive aimed at driving westwards from the Egyptian border to link up with the besieged garrison of Tobruk. His intelligence supposed that this attack would take place around the beginning of October. To find out more information about British intentions, Rommel ordered a reconnaissance in force – Operation *Sommernachtstraum* – across the frontier by elements of the 21. Panzer-Division to determine the state of British readiness. He hoped to locate and capture British supply dumps and to interfere with any build-up that was taking place. The raid was only a partial success, for the move, which started on 14 September, was quickly detected by the Allied armoured car screen and subjected to a good deal of long-range shelling and attacks by the RAF. No sign of a British build-up was found; neither were any supply dumps overrun. On 16 September the force withdrew, leaving Rommel with the opinion that the British were nowhere near being ready to launch a new offensive. This belief was reinforced by the study of documents captured during the operation. They implied that a retreat to the Mersa Matruh area was being considered. In fact, the orders related to a temporary unit withdrawal, not a large-scale strategic realignment. If his forces had penetrated just a little further into Egypt they would have found that a massive British build-up actually was under way, as Auchinleck stockpiled men and *matériel* ready for his forthcoming offensive.

With the immediate threat from the British now appearing to diminish, Rommel could give more of his attention to the problem of Tobruk. The capture of the port would help shorten his supply lines and bring other advantages, for there would no longer be an enemy garrison in his rear as he faced towards Egypt. An added bonus would be the use of those of his formations that were occupied keeping the British holed up in Tobruk, for they would then be available for offensive operations. He saw the whole strategic situation changing in his favour once the question of Tobruk had been settled.

Things were seen differently in Rome and Berlin. Higher authority urged caution, believing that the overall situation, especially with regard to supplies, would improve in the spring of 1942 to a point where the capture of the port would be much easier to accomplish. The Italians felt that the main objective now was to crush the forthcoming British attack, rather than to risk allowing the British to get the upper hand by failing to concentrate forces against them. Rommel decided to override the opinions of his superiors.

Rommel's main problem was one of supply. This lack of reinforcements, equipment, fuel and stores now began to delay his plans. In the previous few months the amount of supplies arriving across the Mediterranean to keep Axis forces sustained had been well below normal requirements. Between June and October 220,000 tons had been lost to British naval and air activity. The problem worried Rommel, but did not deter him from trying to seize Tobruk. He believed that the attack could be hazardous to his overall command, but the prize was well worth the risk. It was just a question of timing. If he attacked first then he was confident he would win; if the British were the first to move then he had to make sure he was prepared to counter them.

Rommel now set out his plans for either eventuality. Before he could attack Tobruk he had to be confident of the line facing the British. It was important that the line should hold up the British should they be the first to attack. He ordered the frontier defences to be strengthened at all the critical places to create a fortified line. Work went ahead at Halfaya, Sidi Omar, Sollum, Capuzzo and Bardia to create strongpoints that could be manned by garrison troops. At Halfaya, the most strategically important position of the line, he placed a mixed command of Germans and Italians which included his *Panzergruppe*'s engineer HQ. The other defended localities were manned by troops of the Italian 55ᵃ Divisione 'Savona'. He located the headquarters of the Afrika Korps near the frontier at Bardia, with 15. Panzer-Division close to Rommel's own HQ at Gambut to the north of the coast road. The 21. Panzer-Division was 32km west of Bardia, near Sidi Azeiz. With these forces in place Rommel was confident that he could deal with an attack. Further back,

German 88mm anti-aircraft gun knocked out during the battle. The powerful gun had a dual use and was employed very effectively in the desert as an anti-tank weapon. Its high silhouette made it somewhat vulnerable to counter-battery fire on the open spaces of the desert – providing that British artillery could get near enough to engage it. (IWM, 7164)

Rommel meets with some of his battalion commanders prior to the British attack. (Western Desert Battlefield Tours)

he had the option of committing the Italian XX Corpo d'Armata if required, but only after obtaining operational authority from Bastico. The two divisions of Gambara's corps were stationed in the desert south of Tobruk, with the 132ª Divisione Corazzata 'Ariete' at Bir El Gubi and the 101ª Divisione Motorizzate 'Trieste' much further to the south-west at Bir Hacheim. Rommel now felt secure and ready for any eventuality. To his front he had the strong defensive forward positions along the frontier backed by two mobile Panzer divisions fairly well forwards. Further back were the two divisions of the Italian XX Corpo d'Armata. He was sure that he would be able to react confidently to any British penetration of the line.

Rommel planned to use the Italian forces of Navarrini's XXI Corpo in the reduction of Tobruk, along with selected German formations as the cutting edge. The four divisions of the Italian corps – 'Brescia', 'Trento', 'Pavia' and 'Bologna' – were already holding the perimeter of the fortress area. Rommel intended that these would support the 15. Panzer-Division and the 90. leichte-Division to make up the attacking force when the time came. He knew that the build-up would take some considerable time and he calculated that he would be ready to strike on 25 November. Up until then, all he could do was continue to build up his strength and pray that the British did not strike first.

OPERATION *CRUSADER*

The war in the desert gave rise to a number of 'private armies' and 'special forces' groups. The main narrative of the campaign rightly concentrates on the major battles and the movement of armies across the wastes of Libya and Egypt, but many other actions took place in the great expanse of desert by small individual groups seeking ways to disrupt the enemy or divert his attention away from the main battle. The period saw the formation of the Long Range Desert Group, the Special Air Service, The Middle East Commandos, 'Popski's Private Army' and several others. Most of their exploits were only mildly successful, many were costly to mount and their effects on the course of the campaign were minimal – no more than pinpricks in the grand order of things. Nonetheless, some of the intelligence gathered behind enemy lines was of great importance to battlefield commanders, and the destruction of enemy fuel dumps and aircraft on the ground added to the sum total of destruction meted out to Rommel's forces. All were undertaken by dedicated and brave men who demonstrated great stamina and ingenuity. Unfortunately, many of them died in exploits that reaped little positive gain other than boosting morale.

Two such attacks took place just before the start of Eighth Army's *Crusader* offensive; neither was successful and many men were lost. The

A British truck moves through the wire on the frontier between Libya and Egypt at the start of the offensive. (IWM, E6686)

The doorway in the villa at Beda Littoria that was thought to house Rommel's headquarters. Lieutenant-Colonel Geoffrey Keyes VC was shot dead here when he and his party burst into the German-held building during the abortive raid by No. 11 Commando just prior to the *Crusader* offensive. (Western Desert Battlefield Tours)

purpose of the operations was to divert Rommel's attention away from the build-up of forces near the border. The first was undertaken by six officers and 53 men of No. 11 Commando, under the command of Lieutenant-Colonel Geoffrey Keyes, with Colonel Robert Laycock accompanying the group as an 'observer'. The group was to land behind enemy lines from submarines near Apollonia and carry out several objectives: firstly, to attack the Italian headquarters at Cyrene and cut all communications; secondly, to do likewise at the Italian Intelligence centre at Apollonia; thirdly, to disrupt all enemy activity around El Faida and, finally, to attack the German headquarters at Beda Littoria and the private villa thought to be occupied by Rommel himself.

The attack on Rommel's house was not the main aim of the raid, but orders suggested that if the German general was present at the villa he was to be captured or killed. The raid began on the night of 13/14 November with Keyes' men attempting to land from two submarines, HMS *Torbay* and HMS *Talisman*. The operation was disrupted from the start, with high seas and strong gale-force winds making disembarkation very difficult. It took some seven hours to get the men ashore in rubber dinghies and canvas canoes from *Torbay*, whilst those in *Talisman* fared even worse with many of the small craft washed off its decks and their crews perished before the submarine abandoned the landings and withdrew with many of the raiders still aboard.

Once ashore, those who had landed reorganized themselves in order to carry out at least some part of their objectives. Keyes and a few men actually made it to the villa two days later, but the Germans inside were alerted and

Keyes was killed in a sharp firefight inside the building. The explosives they carried to demolish the building proved to be too wet to explode and the party withdrew to the planned assembly point leaving their dead commander, two dead Germans and several wounded comrades. A rendezvous was later made with Col. Laycock on the beach, but the party was unable to make contact with the submarine *Torbay* lying just offshore. So the 22 men who had gathered there split up into small groups and tried to march back to the British lines with only a blown enemy dump and three Germans killed as a result of their labours. Only Col. Laycock and Sergeant Terry eventually made it back to safety, 41 days later. Lieutenant-Colonel Keyes was posthumously awarded the Victoria Cross for his part in the operation.

The second diversionary operation was carried out on the night of 16 November, two days before *Crusader* was launched. Led by Captain David Sterling, 'L' Detachment, 1st Special Service Brigade (the unit that subsequently became 1st SAS Regiment) planned to parachute onto the area around Gazala–Tmimi to attack enemy aircraft dispersed on the airfield. Five Bombay aircraft took off from a landing strip near Fuka carrying 57 men on the operation. Unfortunately, the weather deteriorated quite rapidly, dispersing the formation of transport aircraft carrying the raiders. Their pilots pressed on with the operation through thick cloud and dropped the parachutists, their weapons and explosives over a wide area. Daylight revealed they had come down so far south of their objective that a continuation of the raid was impossible. There was nothing for it but to cancel the attack, and for the 22 men who had survived the drop to set off across the desert and try to rendezvous with the vehicles of the Long Range Desert Group, which would take them back to the British lines. It was not an auspicious beginning for the famous SAS Regiment on this its first operation.

The Bristol Blenheim light bomber saw service with the RAF's Western Desert Air Force during *Crusader* both in its conventional role and on ground reconnaissance missions. (IWM, CM1691)

THE BRITISH ATTACK

Operation *Crusader* rolled forwards during the early hours of 18 November. The weather had suddenly deteriorated into a period of thunderstorms and torrential rain, accompanied by falling temperatures and showers of icy cold sleet and strong winds. This made the approach of Eighth Army's strike force to the starting point a miserable affair. Transport laboured through sand turned to mud by the downpours, their drivers struggling relentlessly in the dark to stay on the rapidly disappearing tracks which snaked across the desert. All aircraft on both sides were grounded by the weather.

First through the wire leading XXX Corps' advance onto the battlefield were the mobile armoured cars of the 7th Armoured Division. On the left the 11th Hussars of 22nd Armoured Brigade moved out into the desert, sweeping down into the area to the south, probing for the enemy. Behind them, leading the move in the centre were the light reconnaissance vehicles of the 4th South African Armoured Car Regiment. On the right, the cars of the 1st King's Dragoon Guards led the way. Behind them the main armour began to lumber forwards, heading north-west in an attempt to bring Rommel's armour to battle. At the same time, XIII Corps closed up on the enemy's frontier positions.

Little was seen of the enemy by XXX Corps, although the wide-sweeping armoured cars did make contact with their opposite numbers on the German side to ensure that news of the British advance was signalled back to Afrika Korps' HQ. The three armoured brigades pressed on over the open desert making for their initial objectives around Gabr Saleh, with 22nd Armoured Brigade in the south, the 7th Support Group and the 7th Armoured Brigade in the centre, and 4th Armoured Brigade in the north. By evening all four formations were almost exactly where Cunningham wanted them to be, ready for the expected counter-attack by the tanks of the Afrika Korps. The commander of Eighth Army now established his advance headquarters in the desert south of Gabr Saleh, ready to direct the great armoured clash that was to come.

On the north of the front, XIII Corps' infantry divisions crossed the wire with the New Zealand and 4th Indian Divisions each pushing a brigade out into the desert before wheeling it north to get behind the Axis defences. Behind the advance, the infantry tanks of the 1st Army Tank Brigade held themselves in readiness to tackle any interference with the moves by enemy armour. Along the whole of Eighth Army's line there was little real opposition to any part of the advance.

Earlier that day Rommel had returned from a short stay in Rome. When the commander of the Afrika Korps, Gen.Lt. Crüwell, reported the British movements to him he suggested that they indicated the start of the long-expected British offensive. Rommel thought otherwise, seeing the moves more as a reconnaissance in force than the start of a major attack. He was expecting that Cunningham would make such a move to divert his attention away from his proposed assault on Tobruk, and told Crüwell that he would not rise to the bait. For the time being Rommel ordered all armoured formations to remain where they were. This was not exactly what the British had planned on.

On the second day of the offensive, 19 November, the British held the initiative, but were not sure how to exploit it. Rommel was not reacting as Cunningham hoped he would. By this time the German commander should

have sent an armoured force against XXX Corps to close off the penetration of his lines. His inaction left the British in something of a quandary. The planned move to the area of Gabr Saleh had little strategic importance; it was merely a ploy to bring the Afrika Korps to battle. The non-appearance of German armour meant that the plan had to be changed, but no one appeared to be sure what it should be changed to.

Major-General Gott, commander of 7th Armoured Division, was loath to see his formation stationary when it clearly had the advantage. His corps commander, Lt. Gen. Norrie was of a similar opinion and Cunningham was persuaded that the division should move towards Tobruk, a move that Rommel could not afford to ignore. Orders were therefore given to advance and screen off the areas around Bir el Gubi and Sidi Rezegh. The 22nd Armoured Brigade on the left was to ensure that the advance was safe from interference by the 132ª Divisione Corazzata 'Ariete' in Bir el Gubi and to protect the left flank of 7th Armoured Brigade as it pushed on towards Sidi Rezegh. The Support Group was to remain in its present position ready to assist the other two brigades as required and the 4th Armoured Brigade was to stay near Gabr Saleh to be ready to protect the left flank of XIII Corps as it attacked the enemy frontier garrisons.

These moves resulted in a splitting of the British armoured force and Cunningham had now lost the overwhelming strength he was counting on with which to defeat the Afrika Korps in the great tank battle that he hoped would take place. Rommel remained impassive to Eighth Army's moves in the southern desert, still at odds with Crüwell regarding the objectives of the British. He told the commander of the Afrika Korps to hold his nerve and remain resolute to ensure that the attack on Tobruk, now timed to take place in just two days, went ahead.

British armoured cars cross a wide expanse of barren desert. The reconnaissance vehicles are widely spaced to reduce the risk of being hit by marauding enemy aircraft. The absence of any identifiable features on the harsh landscape made navigation difficult. (IWM, CM2202)

The opening moves of 18 and 19 November

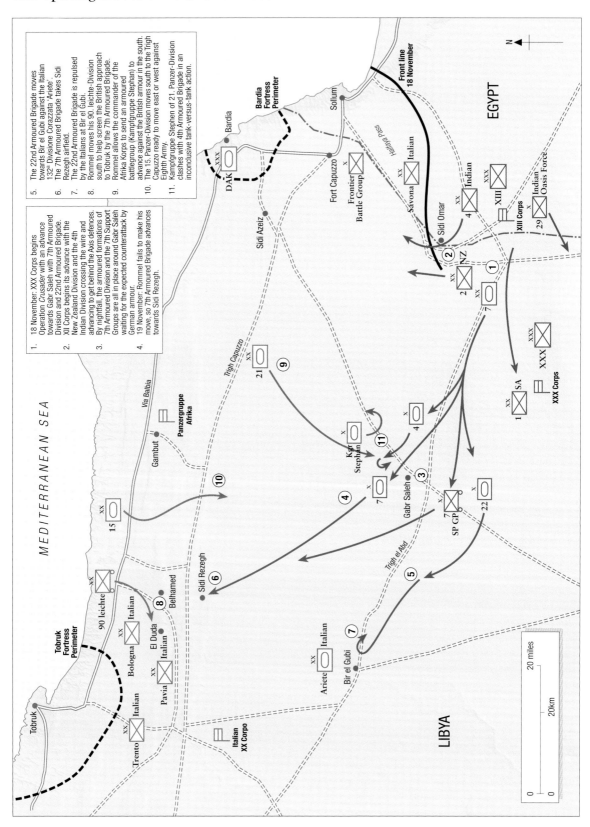

1. 18 November: XXX Corps begins Operation *Crusader* with an advance towards Gabr Saleh with 7th Armoured Division and 22nd Armoured Brigade. XII Corps begins its advance with the New Zealand Division and the 4th Indian Division crossing the wire and advancing to get behind the Axis defences.

2. By nightfall, the armoured formations of 7th Armoured Division and the 7th Support Groups are all in place around Gabr Saleh waiting for the expected counterattack by German armour.

3. 19 November: Rommel fails to make his move, so 7th Armoured Brigade advances towards Sidi Rezegh.

4.

5. The 22nd Armoured Brigade moves towards Bir el Gubi against the Italian 132ª Divisione Corazzata 'Ariete'.

6. The 7th Armoured Brigade takes Sidi Rezegh airfield.

7. The 22nd Armoured Brigade is repulsed by the Italians at Bir el Gubi.

8. Rommel moves his 90. leichte-Division south to help screen the British approach to Tobruk by the 7th Armoured Brigade.

9. Rommel allows the commander of the Afrika Korps to send an armoured battlegroup (Kampfgruppe Stephan) to advance against the British armour in the south.

10. The 15. Panzer-Division moves south to the Trigh Capuzzo ready to move east or west against Eighth Army.

11. Kampfgruppe Stephen of 21. Panzer-Division clashes with 4th Armoured Brigade in an inconclusive tank-versus-tank action.

An enemy minefield is blown up by British sappers before the start of the battle. (IWM, E6169)

When 22nd Armoured Brigade approached Bir el Gubi it brushed up against the outposts of the 132ᵃ Divisione Corazzata 'Ariete'. The Italian formation was known to be located there and was thought to pose a significant threat to any further advance towards Sidi Rezegh. Brigadier Scott-Cockburn was now ordered to attack the 132ᵃ Divisione Corazzata 'Ariete'. He was told to use his untried formation to remove this threat and enable 7th Armoured Brigade to continue towards the area south of Tobruk. The 1st South African Brigade would then come up in support and secure Bir el Gubi, releasing 22nd Armoured Brigade back to the main positions at Gabr Saleh or to wherever its armour was required.

The three Yeomanry regiments that made up 22nd Armoured Brigade (2nd Royal Gloucestershire Horse, and the 3rd and 4th County of London Yeomanry) were newly arrived in the theatre. They were supported with just one regiment of 25-pdr field guns and one troop of anti-tank guns. Major-General Gott thought that an action against the Italians would be a good introduction to desert warfare before the brigade came up against the more formidable German units. Morale was high just after midday as the cavalry squadrons in their brand new Crusader tanks raced across the stony wastes to close with the enemy. The first rush of armour against the widely spaced Italian covering positions swept all before them. As they moved on closer to the division's anti-tank screen, however, they ran into the fire of guns placed in a strong defensive line. The barrage of fire they met soon began to take a toll on the British tanks. A second battalion was ordered into the battle as more and more Crusaders were disabled by shell and shot, or were blown up in the minefields that surrounded the defences. A third battalion went to give its help to the attack only to suffer the same losses as the other two. The attack was costly to the British, but the Italians also suffered and many of their tanks and guns succumbed to the 22nd Armoured Brigade. By the early afternoon it was clear that the 132ᵃ Divisione Corazzata 'Ariete' was too well dug in to be overwhelmed by tanks alone. The attack needed the support of more infantry and more artillery to evict the enemy. Brigadier Scott-Cockburn called a halt to the proceedings and his brigade withdrew to lick its wounds

Matilda tanks of the 4th Royal Tank Regiment from 32nd Army Tank Brigade on the move up to the front. (IWM, E6600)

and count the cost of its first action; 25 of its 136 tanks were lost, with the Italians having suffered 34 of their tanks destroyed along with 15 damaged and the loss of 12 of their guns.

Further to the north, Brigadier Davy's 7th Armoured Brigade had advanced almost to Sidi Rezegh without being confronted by any of the enemy other than some armoured cars from Aufklärungs-Abteilung 33 (motorisiert). The brigade soon reached the southern escarpment that sloped down before Sidi Rezegh. On the floor of the valley was an airfield complete with a large number of Italian aircraft, their ground crews oblivious to the arrival of the British.

Brigadier Davy soon had armoured cars and Crusaders from the 6th Royal Tank Regiment sweeping down from the heights into the valley, strafing the enemy aircraft parked helplessly on the ground. Those that tried to take off were mercilessly shot down and those that were unable to move were blasted by guns or crushed under the tracks of the charging tanks. Within a very short time the airfield was taken and a squadron of tanks pushed on to crest the main northern escarpment at Sidi Rezegh on the other side of the valley. Here they stumbled on outposts of the German 90. leichte-Division in their well-established defensive positions. With no infantry to support them, the Crusaders were forced to move back down into the valley. Other tanks tried to move westwards towards the track that ran up from Bir el Gubi to El Adem, but these too met the dug-in infantry of the Italian 17ᵃ Divisione 'Pavia' and turned back. By nightfall, this success in the north had led XXX Corps commander Lt. Gen. Norrie to begin moving the 7th Armoured Division's Support Group up to join the 7th Armoured Brigade along the valley floor.

The sudden arrival of British tanks at Sidi Rezegh now made the enemy troops surrounding Tobruk seem vulnerable. The 90. leichte-Division holding the northern escarpment was particularly badly placed for there was little German armour within striking distance of the British on the airfield. The division's commander, Gen.Maj. Sümmermann, called for reinforcements and

a number of 100mm guns were rushed down from Bardia on the coast together with a battalion of Italian infantry of the 25ᵃ Divisione 'Bologna' and a battalion of German engineers.

This latest advance by Eighth Army was again seen by Gen.Lt. Crüwell at his headquarters as something more than mere diversionary tactics by the British. The commander of 21. Panzer-Division, Gen.Lt. von Ravenstein, agreed with him and was becoming a little anxious about British moves to the south of his formation. When news of 7th Armoured Brigade's advance onto the escarpment south of Sidi Rezegh reached Rommel, he began to have second thoughts about the reasons behind all this British activity. He gave Crüwell permission for an armoured *Kampfgruppe* from 21. Panzer-Division to destroy the enemy threat in the south. Oberstleutnant Stephan was ordered to take his Panzer-Regiment 5, reinforced with 12 105mm howitzers and four 88mm anti-tank guns, to confront the enemy near Gabr Saleh.

The advancing Germans met the Stuart tanks of Brigadier Gatehouse's 4th Armoured Brigade, less elements of the 3rd and 5th RTRs which were supporting some armoured cars to the north-west, in the late afternoon. Kampfgruppe Stephan with its mix of Panzer IIIs and Panzer IVs and a few Panzer IIs, 85 tanks in total, was more or less matched in numbers by 4th Armoured Brigade's remaining tanks. The two sides now met each other in the first large-scale tank-versus-tank clash in open desert of the war.

The Germans moved into the battle with their anti-tank guns behind them and the British advancing to meet them. The speed of the British tanks took them right into the German lines to fight a close-quarters action in which their inferior main armament was less of a handicap. Order was soon lost and the battle became a tank-stalking-tank encounter, with each side inextricably mixed up with the other. The area was soon engulfed in smoke and dust, which lessened the deadly effect of the German anti-tank guns. The fight raged on through the afternoon with neither side in complete control of its own forces. As the day wore on and the light began to fade, the Germans withdrew to join up with a support column that had arrived to their rear to

Polish troops of the 1st Carpathian Brigade pose for the cameraman after arriving in Tobruk as part of the port's defence force. (IWM, E6045)

refuel and to resupply their forces. The British were kept at arm's length by a screen of anti-tank guns, unable to interfere with the static enemy vehicles through a lack of support from their own artillery. The 4th Armoured Brigade then retired southwards and left the battlefield to the enemy.

As soon as they had left, German engineers came forwards to recover their damaged Panzers whilst those immobile tanks of Eighth Army were destroyed to prevent their reuse. Not all of the British damaged tanks had been left behind, however, for some were towed away for repair. Nonetheless, some 24 Stuarts had been put out of action in the battle. The Germans claimed that their losses were two Panzer IIIs and one Panzer II destroyed and four damaged Panzer IIIs, which were recovered; the British claimed they had knocked out 24 of them, an exaggeration that was to have later repercussions.

It had been a day of mixed fortunes for XXX Corps. Two of its armoured brigades had clashed with the enemy with some losses and incomplete victories, whilst the other armoured brigade had made a successful penetration to the north-west which placed it and the Support Group on the edge of the enemy line surrounding Tobruk. Brigadier Gatehouse was pleased with the performance of his 4th Armoured Brigade as he felt that the Stuart tank was capable of matching those of the enemy, inflicting as many losses to the enemy Panzers as it had received. He was confident that when the 3rd and 5th RTRs had returned to his formation the next day his concentrated brigade would be enlarged by a further 100 or more tanks and be more than a match for the enemy forces in front of him. For Cunningham the day had again proved to be indecisive. Rommel's reaction had been minimal with just one *Kampfgruppe* of armour sent against his forces. The proposed tank battle was yet to materialize, which was most likely a good thing, for Cunningham had lost the concentration of his tanks by allowing two of his armoured brigades to be sent to diverse locations. The original plan for *Crusader* would now have to be rethought.

The third day of the British offensive, 20 November, saw Rommel considering a slight reappraisal of the situation. He now agreed that the British moves were more than a diversion and were an attempt to interfere with his forthcoming attack on Tobruk, timed to start at dawn the next day. Rommel therefore ordered Crüwell to destroy the marauding British armour before it could hinder his own planned operation against the British fortress. The commander of the Afrika Korps decided to use both of his armoured divisions for the task, planning to isolate the forward elements of Eighth Army. He ordered 15. Panzer-Division to advance eastwards from the Gambut area to Sidi Azeiz, whilst the 21. Panzer-Division drove south towards Gabr Saleh to engage the British armour there. His plan was to encircle the British to the west and cut off supply and escape routes to the east. Rather than engage in a full-scale tank battle as Cunningham had hoped, Crüwell was planning to eliminate each of the British armoured columns in turn.

That same day the 7th Armoured Brigade, ensconced on the airfield at Sidi Rezegh, came under attack by a reinforced German 90. leichte-Division. The addition of heavy artillery to the division on the northern escarpment had allowed the Germans to shell the British below them on the valley floor. Sümmermann also launched a counter-attack against the airfield, but this attempt to dislodge 7th Armoured Brigade was repulsed with little difficulty. The continual shelling did, however, prove to be a nuisance to the South African armoured cars, which dispersed for their own safety. The German activity persuaded Brig. Davy that he would need adequate infantry support before making any further attacks on the ridge opposite.

These moves were of course unknown to Cunningham that morning. Reports received by him suggested something quite the opposite. The enemy appeared to be making a general move to the west, as indeed some of its forces were, readying themselves for the forthcoming attack on Tobruk. Major-General Gott at Sidi Rezegh indicated that the enemy in front of him was weak and suggested that the Support Group could be used to make contact with the Tobruk garrison if 70th Division broke out of the encirclement to meet it. The idea seemed attractive, but would go against the original plan of first bringing the enemy's armour to battle and defeating it.

These proposals were considered by Cunningham and agreed to. Major-General Scobie would attack out of the Tobruk perimeter towards the area of El Duda with his 70th Division at dawn on 21 November. The Support Group from 7th Armoured Division would drive north-west at the same time to join up with it, assisted by the 1st South African Division's 5th Brigade. The division's other brigade, the 1st, would remain near Bir el Gubi screening off the Italian 132ᵃ Divisione Corazzata 'Ariete'. The moves had the effect of dispersing more and more of XXX Corps before the German armour had been brought to battle. This was not part of the *Crusader* plan and Cunningham was gradually losing the initiative.

In the meantime, Crüwell's two Panzer divisions of the Afrika Korps were slowly moving eastwards. They found nothing but armoured cars in their path, indicating that the British had the bulk of their forces to the south. Late in the afternoon the 21. Panzer-Division stopped to refuel and to rejoin Kampfgruppe Stephan. The 15. Panzer-Division was ordered to wheel southwards and continue towards Gabr Saleh, with the 21. Panzer-Division following on during

Brigadier Arthur Willison, Commander 32nd Army Tank Brigade, briefs tank crews on how he plans to execute the armoured thrust during the breakout battle from Tobruk. The brigadier uses a sand table to show the terrain over which they will fight and indicates the expected Axis positions that will have to be captured. (IWM, E6850)

the night. Cunningham was now about to get his wish; the Afrika Korps was coming to meet him at Gabr Saleh as he had originally desired, but now only one of his three armoured brigades would be there to receive it.

Fortunately, news of the impending German attack was received during the day through message intercepts. Norrie was informed that the two German divisions would be in the vicinity of Gabr Saleh to attack 4th Armoured Brigade the next day. He immediately gave orders for the 22nd Armoured Brigade to move across from Bir el Gubi to join Gatehouse's brigade east of Gabr Saleh. This would at least allow two armoured brigades, consisting of six battalions of tanks, to match the four battalions of Panzers in the two German Panzer divisions. It was not quite the overwhelming force that was in the original plan as the 7th Armoured Brigade and the Support Group were at Sidi Rezegh, but it was at least a small measure of superiority to help raise confidence in the outcome. In the event, the action consisted of just one British brigade against just one Panzer regiment.

The 15. Panzer-Division was the first to arrive and its Panzer-Regiment 8, supported by two infantry battalions and a powerful artillery force, made contact with 4th Armoured Brigade before 22nd Armoured Brigade had joined up. The action that followed was inconclusive, although both sides were eventually deceived by its outcome. The 4th Armoured Brigade held the best ground and had good defensive positions on a slight rise, which gave them an advantage. The 'hull down' positions of their tanks during the initial clash matched the superiority of the enemy tanks to create, for a while, something of an equal struggle. Gradually, however, the Panzers and their

supporting guns began to push the British back down the reverse of their slope before the light began to fade. About this time, elements of 22nd Armoured Brigade arrived and, fearing a strong flank attack, the Germans withdrew to form a defensive leaguer for the night, recovering their damaged tanks and arranging the replenishment of fuel and ammunition.

News of the action with Eighth Army's armour was met with delight at Crüwell's headquarters, especially as the reports suggested that the British had been pushed right back with considerable losses. The two British brigades had in fact withdrawn across the Trigh el Abd track to regroup and restock their supplies, but the enemy thought that they had been sufficiently harshly dealt with to put them out of action for a long time. The British had lost 26 tanks that day with a roughly equal number of Panzers destroyed or damaged.

At the headquarters of Panzergruppe Afrika, Rommel was having another rethink. News broadcast on Cairo's radio told the world that a renewed and enlarged Eighth Army had launched an attack that was intending to drive through Cyrenaica and Tripolitania to destroy all Axis forces in North Africa. Details were also arriving of the moves by Oasis Group in the southern desert and reports showed that a vast train of British vehicles was advancing through Jarabub and Jalo, possibly heading for Benghazi to cut the Axis supply route. Rommel now agreed with the commander of the Afrika Korps that the British had launched their offensive with a well-equipped and enlarged army. He now knew that he was dealing with a concerted assault by Eighth Army which if not quickly overwhelmed would, eventually, gain the upper hand through its formidable administration chain and shorter supply routes. The assault on Tobruk would have to be postponed and his whole attention was now turned over to defeating the British in the field. He would, nonetheless, maintain the siege of Tobruk for as long as possible. He would also hold the frontier positions whilst he attacked and destroyed the strung-out British forces. With the British 4th Armoured Brigade dealt with, or so he believed, he ordered Gen.Lt. Crüwell immediately to turn his two Panzer divisions around and send them north-west to eliminate the British forces gathering around Sidi Rezegh.

The area around El Duda as it is today. The position at El Duda was the meeting point of the New Zealand 2nd Division and British 70th Division after the breakout from the Tobruk fortress area. (Western Desert Battlefield Tours)

In Cunningham's camp news of the fight between 4th Armoured Brigade and the Afrika Korps was awaited nervously. If Gatehouse's force was badly mauled it would leave the right flank of XXX Corps open and pose a great risk to XIII Corps if the Panzers decided to move north-east against Lt. Gen. Godwin-Austen's infantry corps. When news arrived that the armoured brigade had not been destroyed and had withdrawn relatively intact along with the 22nd Armoured Brigade, Cunningham's spirits lifted immediately. Confidence rose even further when aerial reconnaissance showed that both Panzer divisions were withdrawing to the north. Cunningham believed that the decisive tank battle had been fought and that he had won it. He ordered both the 4th and 22nd Armoured Brigades to pursue the fleeing enemy and attack it relentlessly. The army commander was sure that things were beginning to swing his way. He ordered the breakout of the Tobruk garrison to go ahead as planned and the link-up with 7th Armoured Division to take place at El Duda.

THE CLASH OF ARMOUR

On 21 November both sides were once again on the move. The Afrika Korps was heading north-west to attack 7th Armoured Brigade in the rear and the 4th and 22nd Armoured Brigades were following on close behind trying to catch up with the German advance. Reports radioed back from the British armour claimed that the Panzer formations were in full retreat. It looked for a while as though Eighth Army had won a famous victory. Cunningham now stepped up his offensive in line with the original *Crusader* plan. He informed Lt. Gen. Godwin-Austen that he could begin more offensive action with his XIII Corps; the New Zealand Division was to head north-west towards Tobruk along the Trigh Capuzzo track and the 4th Indian Division was ordered to get behind the enemy's static formations holding the frontier.

This euphoria at Cunningham's HQ was not to last for too long (just a day or two more), but it did continue for long enough for more miscalculations to be made. To the north-west the breakout battle was under way as Maj. Gen. Scobie's beleaguered garrison looked to fight its way out of the

The breakout from Tobruk, 20/21 November

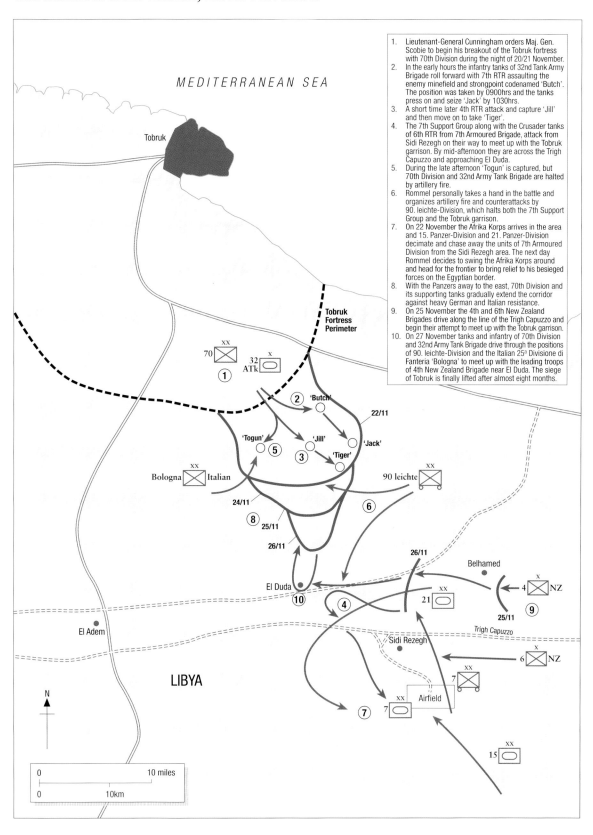

MEDITERRANEAN SEA

Tobruk

Tobruk Fortress Perimeter

1. Lieutenant-General Cunningham orders Maj. Gen. Scobie to begin his breakout of the Tobruk fortress with 70th Division during the night of 20/21 November.
2. In the early hours the infantry tanks of 32nd Tank Army Brigade roll forward with 7th RTR assaulting the enemy minefield and strongpoint codenamed 'Butch'. The position was taken by 0900hrs and the tanks press on and seize 'Jack' by 1030hrs.
3. A short time later 4th RTR attack and capture 'Jill' and then move on to take 'Tiger'.
4. The 7th Support Group along with the Crusader tanks of 6th RTR from 7th Armoured Brigade, attack from Sidi Rezegh on their way to meet up with the Tobruk garrison. By mid-afternoon they are across the Trigh Capuzzo and approaching El Duda.
5. During the late afternoon 'Togun' is captured, but 70th Division and 32nd Army Tank Brigade are halted by artillery fire.
6. Rommel personally takes a hand in the battle and organizes artillery fire and counterattacks by 90. leichte-Division, which halts both the 7th Support Group and the Tobruk garrison.
7. On 22 November the Afrika Korps arrives in the area and 15. Panzer-Division and 21. Panzer-Division decimate and chase away the units of 7th Armoured Division from the Sidi Rezegh area. The next day Rommel decides to swing the Afrika Korps around and head for the frontier to bring relief to his besieged forces on the Egyptian border.
8. With the Panzers away to the east, 70th Division and its supporting tanks gradually extend the corridor against heavy German and Italian resistance.
9. On 25 November the 4th and 6th New Zealand Brigades drive along the line of the Trigh Capuzzo and begin their attempt to meet up with the Tobruk garrison.
10. On 27 November tanks and infantry of 70th Division and 32nd Army Tank Brigade drive through the positions of 90. leichte-Division and the Italian 25ᵃ Divisione di Fanteria 'Bologna' to meet up with the leading troops of 4th New Zealand Brigade near El Duda. The siege of Tobruk is finally lifted after almost eight months.

70 xx
32 ATk x
(1)

(2) 'Butch'
22/11
'Jack'
'Togun' 'Jill'
(5) (3)
'Tiger'
Bologna xx Italian
90 leichte xx
24/11
(6)
(8) 25/11
26/11
26/11
Belhamed
El Duda
(10) (4) 21 xx
4 x NZ
(9)
25/11
El Adem
Trigh Capuzzo
LIBYA
Sidi Rezegh
6 x NZ
7 xx
N
xx Airfield
(7) 7
15 xx

0   10 miles
0   10km

encirclement and meet up with 7th Armoured Brigade. It was hoped that the two forces would meet at El Duda at around 1600hrs. Sappers had worked through the night to clear minefields, move barbed wire and erect four bridges over the anti-tank ditch in front of the advance. At dawn the attack began with infantry supported by the slow, ponderous Matilda tanks of the 32nd Army Tank Brigade. Ahead of them were a number of strongpoints thought to be held by Italian troops of the 25ᵃ Divisione 'Bologna', but which were in fact held by the German 90. leichte-Division. The assault began well and then gradually fell behind schedule until it reached a point where the advancing troops were forced to a halt and defend the gains made earlier in the day. Opposition was greater than expected and the proposed meet-up with 7th Armoured Brigade was postponed until the next day, leaving the night to be spent consolidating the corridor the division had carved into the German perimeter.

A few kilometres to the south-east, Brig. Davy's brigade was not itself in a position to meet up with the breakout from Tobruk, for it had become involved in its own vicious struggle with the German 90. leichte-Division. The day started with an attack by 7th Support Group and a squadron of tanks on the northern escarpment seeking to get through to the Trigh Capuzzo and then to sweep along the track to El Duda with the Support Group following on. The action opened with an infantry attack against the German-held ridge, which was seized after a very difficult struggle. This minor success was immediately followed by an ominous warning that a great number of enemy tanks was heading straight for Sidi Rezegh from the south-east. The two divisions of the Afrika Korps were arriving in the area after their forced march up from Gabr Saleh.

Major-General Gott was now put in a very difficult position, for the Tobruk breakout was under way and it was imperative that he press on with his two brigades to meet up with it. It was also crucial that he deal with the Panzer threat in his rear. Gott decided that Brigadier 'Jock' Campbell should carry on with the attack to join up with the 70th Division with the bulk of his Support Group and the 6th RTR, whilst the other two tank battalions of 7th Armoured Brigade, the 7th Queen's Own Hussars and the 2nd RTR, and the remainder of the Support Group turned around and dealt with the German Panzers.

Brigadier Campbell's attack partially succeeded, for the infantry managed to gain the Trigh Capuzzo track and hold onto it. The tanks of 6th RTR fared less well, for as the regiment crossed over the track and passed Sidi Rezegh, its tanks were hit by German and Italian anti-tank guns. This artillery was sited to bring their fire against both that advance and any movement out of the 3,600m corridor opened up by 70th Division. Rommel was organizing the fire of these guns in person, having come forwards from his HQ at Gambut to observe the battle for himself. When the disastrous advance was eventually halted, the 6th RTR found that its tank strength had been reduced to just 28 runners.

Down on the valley floor a depleted 7th Armoured Brigade was readying itself for the onslaught that was about to descend on it from the south-east. It was somewhat bolstered by the news that the 4th and 22nd Armoured Brigades were racing northwards to meet up with it, but for the moment it would have to deal with the German armour on its own.

With all this movement across the desert by both sides, an extraordinary situation had arisen. The British Official History of the campaign noted the

complicated and confused nature of the fighting: 'Over the twenty or so miles [32km] of country from the front of the Tobruk sortie to the open desert to the south-east of Sidi Rezegh airfield, the forces of both sides were sandwiched like layers of a Neapolitan ice.' From north to south there were: the British 70th Division in the corridor facing south, the Italian 25ᵃ Divisione 'Bologna' and German 90. leichte-Division facing both north and south, the Support Group of 7th Armoured Division facing north, the 7th Armoured Division facing south, the 15. Panzer-Division and 21. Panzer-Division facing north and the 4th and 22nd Armoured Divisions facing north behind them. It is not surprising then that when the opposing sides clashed, confusion reigned, with neither side knowing which was the front and which was the rear.

When the German Panzers eventually struck Brig. Davy's brigade on the valley floor it soon became clear to him that the whole of the Afrika Korps was pitted against his two tank battalions and one regiment of field artillery. The shock of the attack hit the 7th Hussars with such ferocity that they soon all but ceased to exist. The German tanks passed right through the armoured brigade and lines of field guns smashing everything in front of them, and then swivelled around and smashed everything to their sides. Smoke, dust and drifting sand obscured the battlefield as the two sides became inextricably linked in battle.

After much close-quarters fighting the Panzers moved off to the eastern end of the valley to refuel, leaving a very battered 7th Hussars to recover as much of their regiment as possible. Only ten of their tanks remained serviceable after the brief but violent action. At the end of the morning the Afrika Korps were on the move again down the valley and along the southern escarpment towards the airfield. This time it was 7th Armoured Brigade's 2nd RTR that felt the full force of their attack. Once again a confused and explosive tank-versus-tank encounter ensued, intermixed with artillery and anti-tank gun fire. The pressure of the assault took the enemy through to

South African-built Marmon-Herrington armoured cars on patrol just after the start of the *Crusader* offensive. During the early years of the war in the desert this type of reconnaissance vehicle was the only one available to the British in sufficient numbers. The vehicle proved to be very reliable over the hostile terrain encountered in North Africa, although it was considered to be under-armed with a Boys anti-tank rifle and a Bren gun as its only offensive weapons. (IWM, E6756)

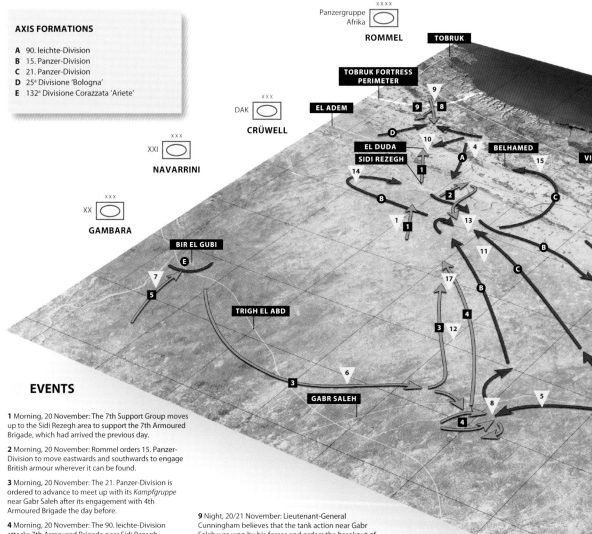

AXIS FORMATIONS

A 90. leichte-Division
B 15. Panzer-Division
C 21. Panzer-Division
D 25ª Divisione 'Bologna'
E 132ª Divisione Corazzata 'Ariete'

Panzergruppe Afrika
ROMMEL

TOBRUK

DAK
CRÜWELL

XXI
NAVARRINI

XX
GAMBARA

TOBRUK FORTRESS PERIMETER

EL ADEM

EL DUDA
SIDI REZEGH

BELHAMED

VIA

BIR EL GUBI

TRIGH EL ABD

GABR SALEH

EVENTS

1 Morning, 20 November: The 7th Support Group moves up to the Sidi Rezegh area to support the 7th Armoured Brigade, which had arrived the previous day.

2 Morning, 20 November: Rommel orders 15. Panzer-Division to move eastwards and southwards to engage British armour wherever it can be found.

3 Morning, 20 November: The 21. Panzer-Division is ordered to advance to meet up with its *Kampfgruppe* near Gabr Saleh after its engagement with 4th Armoured Brigade the day before.

4 Morning, 20 November: The 90. leichte-Division attacks 7th Armoured Brigade near Sidi Rezegh, but is beaten back.

5 Afternoon, 20 November: The 15. Panzer-Division moves south to attack 4th Armoured Brigade whilst the 21. Panzer-Division regroups and refuels to the north.

6 Afternoon, 20 November: Warned about the moves of the Panzer divisions, Lt. Gen. Norrie shifts the 22nd Armoured Brigade across from Bir el Gubi to join up with 4th Armoured Brigade near Gabr Saleh to meet the expected German attack.

7 Afternoon, 20 November: The 1st South African Brigade moves to take over the positions left by 22nd Armoured Brigade and engage the Italian 132ª Divisione Corazzata 'Ariete' at Bir el Gubi.

8 Late afternoon, 20 November: 15. Panzer-Division meets the prepared positions held by 4th Armoured Brigade in a tank-versus-tank battle. The German Panzers gain the upper hand and 4th Armoured Brigade withdraws just as the 22nd Armoured Brigade arrives in the area. The 15. Panzer-Division's commander thinks that he is being outflanked and orders a withdrawal to the north.

9 Night, 20/21 November: Lieutenant-General Cunningham believes that the tank action near Gabr Saleh was won by his forces and orders the breakout of the fortress area at Tobruk to begin. In the early hours, Maj. Gen. Scobie's 70th Division and the tanks of 32nd Army Tank Brigade begin to attack the Axis ring around the port. The moves are resisted by the Italian 25ª Divisione 'Bologna' and by 90. leichte-Division.

10 Morning, 21 November: The 7th Support Group attacks towards Tobruk to meet up with the units attempting the break out. It immediately runs into heavy resistance from the German 90. leichte-Division.

11 Morning, 21 November: Both German Panzer divisions drive north-west to attack British units around Sidi Rezegh.

12 Cunningham sees the German Panzer movements as a withdrawal away from his armour at Gabr Saleh and orders the 4th and 22nd Armoured Brigades to follow in pursuit and destroy the enemy.

13 Late morning, 21 November: The Panzer divisions hit the 7th Armoured Brigade with great force. During some hours of heavy fighting the British armoured formation is badly mauled and dispersed.

14 Afternoon, 21 November: The tanks of 15. Panzer-Division drive westwards to refuel and then turn to attack 7th Support Group. Once again the Panzers have the upper hand and disperse Brig. Campbell's brigade.

15 Late afternoon, 21 November: Gen.Lt. Crüwell is concerned at the approach of the 4th and 22nd Armoured Brigades and orders the 21. Panzer-Division to retire towards the 90. leichte-Division near Belhamed for the night.

16 Late afternoon, 21 November: The 15. Panzer-Division drives eastwards into the desert to leaguer for the night.

17 Evening, 21 November: The 4th and 22nd Armoured Brigades make slow progress on their drive up from Gabr Saleh and stop for the night well short of Sidi Rezegh, unable to take any part in the day's fighting.

THE FIRST ARMOURED BATTLE BETWEEN BRITISH AND GERMAN FORCES OF THE WAR, 20/21 NOVEMBER

Both 15. and 21. Panzer-Divisionen counter the British 22nd and 4th Armoured Brigades then move west to attack 7th Support Brigade from the rear at Sidi Rezegh.

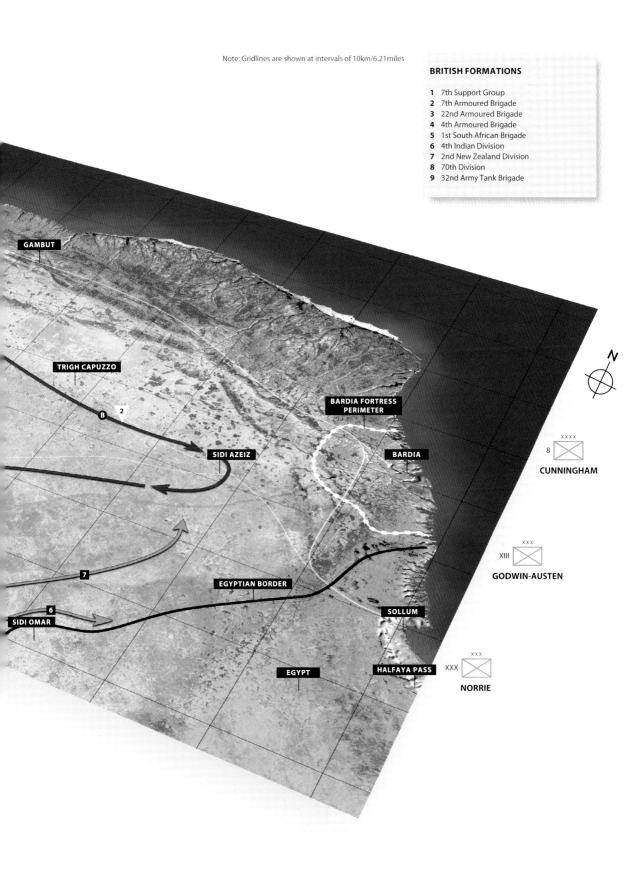

Note: Gridlines are shown at intervals of 10km/6.21miles

BRITISH FORMATIONS

1 7th Support Group
2 7th Armoured Brigade
3 22nd Armoured Brigade
4 4th Armoured Brigade
5 1st South African Brigade
6 4th Indian Division
7 2nd New Zealand Division
8 70th Division
9 32nd Army Tank Brigade

GAMBUT

TRIGH CAPUZZO

B 2

SIDI AZEIZ

BARDIA FORTRESS
PERIMETER

BARDIA

8 XXXX
CUNNINGHAM

7

EGYPTIAN BORDER

6

SIDI OMAR

XIII XXX
GODWIN-AUSTEN

SOLLUM

EGYPT

HALFAYA PASS XXX XXX
NORRIE

51

those units of the Support Group still on the valley floor and the battle raged throughout the day until the weight of British artillery fire and a shortage of ammunition and fuel forced the Panzers and their supporting infantry to retire for the night. The resistance put up by the Support Group had prevented the Germans achieving their objective of driving through the whole length of the valley to meet up with friendly forces at El Duda.

The day had turned out to be one of devastation for two of the brigades of 7th Armoured Division. The Support Group and 7th Armoured Brigade had suffered heavy losses in men, tanks and artillery. The other two brigades of XXX Corps, the 4th and 22nd Armoured Brigades, had not taken part in any of the actions, for they had taken twice as long as the two German Panzer divisions to cover the ground up from Gabr Saleh. Those formations fighting in the Sidi Rezegh area had seen little of them during the day, but their presence in the locality at nightfall led to some concerns in the enemy camp.

The day of 21 November had been a successful one for Rommel. He had personally helped stall the breakout of the Tobruk garrison and his Panzer forces had heaped great destruction upon the 7th Armoured Division opposing him across the divide between the northern and southern escarpments at Sidi Rezegh. Nonetheless, he was concerned by the fact that he seemed to have his Panzers in a position that was sandwiched between a growing number of British forces and much enemy armour. He was also aware that the British still had a whole corps of infantry waiting near the frontier to join in the battle. He knew that once the fighting had been reduced to a slogging match, infantry would be the key to success. The area around Sidi Rezegh was not open desert and the possession of the two escarpments by infantry, especially the northern one so close to the defenders of Tobruk, could decide the outcome of the whole battle.

Rommel's plans for the next day, 22 November, centred on containing the sortie by the Tobruk garrison and taking back the whole of the northern escarpment. He decided that the 15. Panzer-Division would withdraw a short distance towards Gambut to regroup whilst the 21. Panzer-Division cleared British forces from the northern escarpment and the airfield in order to advance to Belhammed. The 15. Panzer-Division would then join in the action from the east.

To the British, the move of the Panzer divisions from the valley and eastern end of the southern escarpment that night after such a hard-fought action to gain this ground had the feel of withdrawal about it. Once again those at XXX Corps and Eighth Army headquarters misread the German moves, leading to another bout of self-congratulations over 'seeing off' the enemy. Only the battered survivors of 7th Armoured Brigade and the Support Group felt that they had not gained any such victory.

For some reason Cunningham received only the good news of that day's action. He was informed that XXX Corps had met and defeated the Afrika Korps, with figures showing that 170 Panzers had been damaged or destroyed – a reduction in Crüwell's tank force of 50 per cent. The 7th Armoured Division's losses were also grave, but Lt. Gen. Norrie still had two other virtually intact armoured brigades in his corps ready to continue the fight. Good news was also coming in from XIII Corps' front. The New Zealand Division had advanced northwards and had one brigade, 6th New Zealand Infantry Brigade, onto the Trigh Capuzzo to the rear of Bardia supported by the Matilda tanks of 1st Army Tank Brigade. The 4th Indian Division was abreast of Freyberg's division to the east, having reached Sidi Omar to begin rolling up the enemy defenders holding the frontier from the rear.

Crüwell's Panzers attacked into the valley the next day, 22 November, and once again hit the remnants of the embattled 7th Armoured and the Support Brigades, this time supported by 22nd Armoured Brigade. Panzer-Regiment 5 with its 57 tanks drove along from the west whilst the 21. Panzer-Division's motorized infantry from Schützen-Regiment 104 hit the British from the north. Again the action was quickly obscured by smoke and dust as the two sides became locked in combat. Tanks were pitted against tanks and guns, and the losses on both sides once again began to mount. In the centre, the guns of the 7th Support Group gave sterling service to the tanks. Again and again they were charged down by enemy Panzers whilst their crews struck steadfastly to their task. Confusion reigned as British tanks withdrew, regrouped and came at the Germans. Some control was exercised in person by the Support Group's commander, Brig. Campbell, who drove back and forth, standing upright in his armoured car with a red flag in his hand, rallying the tanks and urging them back into action.

The airfield became strewn with vehicle wrecks, burning tanks and smashed guns. As the afternoon wore on the Support Group's infantry and artillery were overrun and disintegrated; the armoured brigades were decimated. The desert war had finally become a war of tank attrition with the Germans gradually gaining the upper hand, although Crüwell's tanks did not escape unscathed from the mêlée for their numbers were also whittled away in the close-quarter encounters. Then came the news that 15. Panzer-Division was on the move, circling round from the south-west towards the battle. Major-General Gott knew that this development could sound the death knell for his division. He decided to disengage his three brigades and ordered them to fall back to the positions held by the 5th South African Brigade near the southern escarpment just as night was falling.

The 4th Armoured Brigade with its 108 tanks had again missed the battle. It was away to the east guarding XXX Corps' left flank from the attentions of 15. Panzer-Division when it was ordered to join the fight on the valley floor. Its most advanced unit, 3rd RTR, arrived just as the withdrawal was taking place. Nonetheless, the redoubtable Brig. Campbell led the first tanks into the attack from his armoured car charging at the enemy Panzers, which were at that moment also retiring to replenish fuel and ammunition. The attack was easily beaten off by Panzer-Regiment 5.

25-PDR FIELD GUNS OF THE 60TH FIELD REGIMENT ROYAL ARTILLERY FROM 7TH SUPPORT GROUP IN ACTION AGAINST GERMAN ARMOUR FROM 21. PANZER-DIVISION AT SIDI REZEGH (p.54–55)

The scene shows the heat of battle and the last-ditch stand made by gunners of the 60th Field Regiment Royal Artillery on the open desert floor. The gunners faced hopeless odds, firing their pieces over open sights trying to counter the mass of German tanks and infantry from the 21. Panzer-Division that swarmed amongst them. Many of the field guns were overwhelmed by the enemy as they stormed through the British positions during the first battle of Sidi Rezegh. At the end of the attack, ten of the 24 guns and their crews had been completely wiped out by the enemy.

The 60th Field Regiment Royal Artillery was a Territorial Army unit raised in the Lincoln and Grimsby areas, nicknamed the 'Lincolnshire Gunners'. The regiment served in France in 1940 and was part of the great evacuation of the British Expeditionary Force at Dunkirk, leaving all its guns immobilized in France. The regiment was later shipped out to Iraq to suppress a revolt and then to Syria where it joined the campaign against the Vichy French. In 1941 it arrived in Egypt to serve with the 7th Support Group of Eighth Army in Operation *Crusader*.

The 25-pdr was the basic field gun used by the British Army throughout the war. The gun had a six-man crew known as a detachment, whose roles were as follows: The 'commander' (1), a sergeant, who made large traverses of the gun and was normally positioned to the rear; the 'rammer' (2) who rammed the ammunition home and operated the breech lever; the 'layer' (3), who sat on the wooden seat on the left-hand side of the gun, adjusted the sights and fired the gun; the 'loader' (4) who loaded the ammunition into the gun; the 'ammunition handler' (5) who passed the shells and charges to the loader and checked the fuses and the 'second-in-command' (6), a corporal, who looked after the ammunition, set the fuses and the charges and was responsible for the movement and braking of the trailer.

The day still had one more shock to lay on the British. Brigadier Gatehouse had left his headquarters at 4th Armoured Brigade just after sunset to attend a conference with Maj. Gen. Gott and the other brigade commanders. The brigade had begun to leaguer for the night and was dispersed to the east of the southern escarpment. Creeping towards these scattered tank battalions, trying to find their way westwards, were the advance units of Panzer-Regiment 8 from Gen.Lt Neumann-Silkow's 15. Panzer-Division. As luck would have it they ran headlong into the headquarters of 4th Armoured Brigade. Within minutes the Panzers had surrounded the tanks and vehicles of the shocked headquarters squadron and forced them to surrender. The brigade's second-in-command, 17 officers and 150 other ranks were captured, along with 35 tanks and all the armoured cars and transport belonging to the headquarters group. To make matters worse, all of the brigade's signals, together with its and XXX Corps' codes, were captured by the enemy. The losses now compromised all radio traffic between corps and divisions. This left 4th Armoured Brigade virtually impotent for almost two days before a new headquarters organzation could be raised and put into action.

Once again the day belonged to the enemy. The tank strength of 7th Armoured Brigade was now down to just ten tanks from the 28 it had at the start of the day. The 22nd Armoured Brigade had been reduced from 79 tanks to just 34. The situation for the enemy was slightly better for it still had 173 Panzers mobile in the field and had retaken the whole of the valley floor.

Things were tight at Sidi Rezegh, but Eight Army had been moving forwards elsewhere on the battlefield. The 70th Division had strengthened its corridor through the enemy surrounding Tobruk, but was told not to progress any further until the situation on the escarpments improved. To the east the New Zealanders were enjoying their advance, having taken Fort Capuzzo, cut the water pipe leading to Bardia and severed all Axis telegraph and telephone cables over a wide area. The 7th Indian Brigade had also been making steady progress around Sidi Omar Nuovo, albeit at some cost to the infantry tanks that supported it. Enemy anti-tank guns had destroyed 37 tanks (mostly Matildas) from the 1st Army Tank Brigade.

News was sparse at Cunningham's headquarters that night. The full scale of the losses suffered by 7th Armoured Division was unknown both at army and corps level. When, just after midnight, nothing had been heard from the

Major-General Gott, Commander 7th Armoured Division (right), with Brig. 'Jock' Campbell VC, Commander 7th Support Group. (IWM, E7401)

First battle of Sidi Rezegh, 22 and 23 November

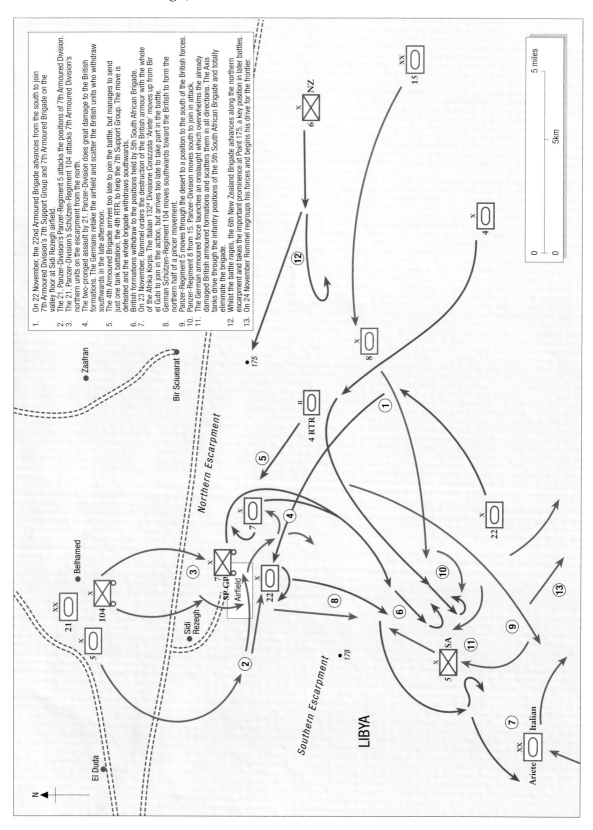

1. On 22 November, the 22nd Armoured Brigade advances from the south to join 7th Armoured Division's 7th Support Group and 7th Armoured Brigade on the valley floor at Sidi Rezegh airfield.
2. The 21. Panzer-Division's Panzer-Regiment 5 attacks the positions of 7th Armoured Division.
3. The 21. Panzer-Division's Schützen-Regiment 104 attacks 7th Armoured Division's northern units on the escarpment from the north.
4. The two-pronged assault by 21. Panzer-Division does great damage to the British formations. The Germans retake the airfield and scatter the British units who withdraw southwards in the late afternoon.
5. The 4th Armoured Brigade arrives too late to join the battle, but manages to send just one tank battalion, the 4th RTR, to help the 7th Support Group. The move is defeated and the whole brigade withdraws southwards.
6. British formations withdraw to the positions held by 5th South African Brigade.
7. On 23 November, Rommel orders the destruction of the British armour with the whole of the Afrika Korps. The Italian 132ª Divisione Corazzata 'Ariete' moves up from Bir el Gubi to join in the action, but arrives too late to take part in the battle.
8. German Schützen-Regiment 104 moves southwards toward the British to form the northern half of a pincer movement.
9. Panzer-Regiment 5 moves through the desert to a position to the south of the British forces.
10. Panzer-Regiment 8 from 15. Panzer-Division moves south to join in attack.
11. The German armoured force launches an onslaught which overwhelms the already damaged British armoured formations and scatters them in all directions. The Axis tanks drive through the infantry positions of the 5th South African Brigade and totally eliminate the brigade.
12. Whilst the battle rages, the 6th New Zealand Brigade advances along the northern escarpment and takes the important prominence at Point 175, a key position in later battles.
13. On 24 November Rommel regroups his forces and begins his drive for the frontier.

58

division, Cunningham gave out orders for the coming day's actions. He believed that events would develop into more of an infantry battle and decided that 22nd Armoured Brigade would move south to Bir el Gubi and relieve the 1st South African Brigade, which would then move up towards Sidi Rezegh during the night to join its sister formation, the 5th South African Brigade. Meanwhile, XIII Corps would continue to push northwards towards Bardia on the coast and the New Zealand Division would move further along the Trigh Capuzzo towards Tobruk, a move which would bring it into contact with the Axis forces holding the northern escarpment.

The enemy were also making plans for the day's fighting on 23 November. Rommel was concerned that his forces away to the east at the frontier were under a great deal of pressure from British XIII Corps, but was unable to offer much help to them until the British around Sidi Rezegh were eliminated. He therefore ordered Crüwell to use the whole of the Afrika Korps to attack towards Bir el Gubi whilst the 132ᵃ Divisione Corazzata 'Ariete' advanced to meet him. The remnants of the 7th Armoured Division would be caught between these two advances and be crushed. Crüwell in fact modified these orders and his change of plan had the two German Panzer divisions, except Schützen-Regiment 104 of 21. Panzer-Division, driving south-west to join forces with the 132ᵃ Divisione Corazzata 'Ariete'. Schützen-Regiment 104 would become the northern force onto which the whole of the Axis armour would drive the British. It was the same encircling and crushing intention as proposed by Rommel, but with a different composition.

The Afrika Korps attacked southwards that day with just the 15. Panzer-Division, for Crüwell was impatient to get the battle moving. Panzer-Regiment 5 was late starting and was told to catch up with the main body as quickly as possible. By 0800hrs the leading elements had driven into the 7th Support Group and scattered its personnel and vehicles across the desert, killing and burning as it went. The Panzers then wheeled to the west to strike the flank of 5th South African Brigade and get amongst the positions of the infantry. The brigade was caught by surprise and it took a while before its field and anti-tank guns all came into action. Great damage was done to the South Africans, but they replied in kind and inflicted losses on the Germans. The Panzers carried on southwards and just after noon joined up with the Italian 132ᵃ Divisione Corazzata 'Ariete' and Panzer-Regiment 5. Some delays

The mosque on the ridge at Sidi Rezegh. The fighting in this area for the possession of the high ground at Sidi Rezegh was severe throughout the whole of the battle. The feature was vital to the relief of Tobruk. (Western Desert Battlefield Tours)

An RAF salvage crew inspect a downed Hurricane fighter to decide whether the damaged aircraft should be cannibalized *in situ* or hauled back to workshops in the rear for repair. (IWM, CM 2231)

forced the attack northwards to be postponed until around 1500hrs, at which time all the Axis tanks rolled forwards en masse. Over 150 Panzers and Italian M13/40s followed by battalions of lorried infantry swept across the desert in a scene reminiscent of a cavalry charge.

This time the South African gun lines were ready for them and greeted the enemy with accurate and sustained shellfire. The fire was effective but not decisive and Axis tanks rolled on into the desert location occupied by the South Africans. Enemy tanks were soon amongst infantry and began their carnage. Some help was given by the 22nd Armoured Brigade but it was just a small effort against the ocean of shell and shot being unleashed by the enemy. The infantry brigade was completely overrun and those men that survived the fighting and were able to surrender did so. The Afrika Korps claimed 3,394 prisoners were taken that day; the 5th South African Brigade ceased to exist as a fighting formation. The 22nd Armoured Brigade lost another 12 of the precious 34 tanks it had had at the start of the day. Generalleutnant Crüwell's formations had also not escaped lightly for around 60 tanks had been knocked out or damaged in the day's fighting, along with appreciable numbers of tank crews and lorried infantry.

Earlier that day, before the full realization of the events which had overtaken 7th Armoured Division and the South Africans became clear at Eighth Army's HQ, Cunningham had visited XIII Corps's headquarters. He decided that Lt. Gen. Godwin-Austen was now to take control of the whole infantry operation to relieve Tobruk. His corps was to bring 70th Division under command and both of the South African brigades just as soon as details of the transfer could be worked out. The relief of Tobruk would now be an infantry operation with XXX Corps' armour tasked with plugging away the enemy tank force. When the army commander arrived back at his command post and was informed of the disaster that had overtaken his armour, he realized that XXX Corps was no longer able to meet the Afrika Korps with any overwhelming force.

That night, Gen. Cunningham was convinced that he had lost the battle. Figures showed that XXX Corps could muster only around 44 tanks, whilst the enemy most likely had almost 150. The superiority in armour upon which the whole of Operation *Crusader* depended had been squandered. Cunningham's spirits were at very low ebb. Since the start of the offensive he had been under extreme pressure. Rommel's reluctance to participate in an armoured battle on the first two days of the offensive had resulted in the initiative gradually slipping from the grasp of Eighth Army's commander. He now saw defeat staring him in the face and reacted in a manner that shocked some at his headquarters. Cunningham decided that the only course left open

A knocked-out German Panzer IV is inspected by a British soldier. One of the tank's crew is lying dead beside it. (IWM, E6734)

to him was to order a withdrawal of Eighth Army back to the frontier behind the defensive minefields and wire from which it came and gave the preliminary orders for this retreat to begin.

This view of the situation was not agreed with by Cunningham's subordinates, and his chief of staff, Brigadier Galloway, felt that he should intervene. On his own initiative, he spoke to the commander-in-chief in Cairo and urged Gen. Auchinleck to come forward to Eighth Army's headquarters as soon as he could. When Auchinleck arrived the next day he was confronted with a situation that was grim in the extreme, but one that careful study showed was not beyond recovery.

Eighth Army was certainly in great danger from Rommel's armoured force, which outnumbered the British by a considerable margin. The German commander could, if he chose, cut off the remains of XXX Corps and then turn on XIII Corps' infantry with the possibility of driving right through to the river Nile. The safest move for the commander-in-chief might be to agree with Cunningham that the battle was lost, break off the offensive and once again adopt a defensive position along the frontier. On the other hand, Auchinleck considered that Rommel was also in a compromised position. His forces were most likely as damaged as Eighth Army's were, for Axis losses, although not as great as the British, were still substantial. There was also the question of his supply situation. By now it was obviously severely stretched and there was still the threat of Tobruk to his rear. If Eighth Army threw its last reserves into the battle and relied on the proven fighting ability of its troops whilst it brought up fresh units from Egypt, the pressure might swing the struggle in favour of the British. Auchinleck decided there and then to rescind Cunningham's decision to pull back and ordered the offensive to continue. His corps and divisional commanders were all in agreement and in favour of carrying on the fight. The move did, however, place a cloud over Cunningham and his handling of the situation, leaving him in a position at the head of Eighth Army that had become virtually untenable.

Auchinleck was adamant that the offensive would still strive for its ultimate goal of the conquest of Cyrenaica and Tripolitania. To do so he thought that the organzation of the forces in contact with the enemy needed changing. He briefed Cunningham on some new proposals and laid out his intentions in a written directive that contained the following passage: 'You will therefore continue to attack the enemy relentlessly using all your resources even to the last tank. Your main object will be as always the destruction of enemy forces.' He suggested that Godwin-Austen should control all formations north of an east–west line through Sidi Azeiz, including the Tobruk garrison, while XIII Corps was to capture El Duda and the Sidi Rezegh ridges, whatever the cost. Lieutenant-General Norrie's XXX Corps was to use its remaining armour to protect the flanks of the battlefield – in particular the 1st South African and the New Zealand Divisions – from attack by enemy Panzers. It was also to screen the enemy from scattered forces and supply dumps in the south-east. These new orders were to take effect at midnight on 24 November.

Meanwhile during that day the 4th and 6th New Zealand Brigades had been edging their way along the Trigh Capuzzo towards Sidi Rezegh and onto the northern ridge, making steady if not spectacular progress. They had even managed to overrun the mobile headquarters of the Afrika Korps and captured over 200 German staff, their vehicles and much of their signalling equipment. Unfortunately for the New Zealand Division, Gen.Lt. Crüwell and his chief of staff, Obstlt. Bayerlein, had left the headquarters some 30 minutes before. Elsewhere that day a lull in the fighting allowed 7th Armoured Brigade to repair and replenish some of their losses and improve the strength of their armoured battalions.

The events at Cunningham's HQ of 24 November marked the end of the first phase of Operation *Crusader*, and it appeared that the great offensive was not turning out to be the success that had been envisaged. The previous seven days had not seen the tank battle that was planned for at the start of the operation, nor had the link-up with Tobruk been achieved. Instead, Eighth

This Matilda tank was captured by the Germans, repainted, and then put back into service by the Afrika Korps. It was later knocked out and recaptured by the British during the *Crusader* battle. (IWM, 7482)

Army tottered on the brink of a great defeat and it would take a great deal of hard and determined fighting to carve out any sort of victory. Fortunately, Auchinleck's determination and a decision made that day by the German commander of Panzergruppe Afrika eventually resulted in the victory that Eighth Army was striving for.

ROMMEL DRIVES EAST

News of XIII Corps' attack on the German and Italian troops holding the frontier disturbed Rommel. For more than two days these troops had withstood the growing pressure being applied by the 4th Indian and New Zealand Divisions. Both of these infantry divisions, supported by the tanks of 1st Army Tank Brigade, were loose behind the Axis lines, picking away at the defences, severing supply lines and cutting contact with the bulk of Panzergruppe Afrika away to the west. There was a limited time they could endure this pressure without some aid being sent to them and Rommel was very aware that time was running out for them. The situation was nowhere near critical, but Rommel felt he must soon do something about it.

The heavy fighting on 23 November spread confusion through both the British and German camps. Generalleutnant Crüwell knew that his losses in tanks were appreciable, but he also knew that it had been worse for Eighth Army. It was not until 0600hrs on 24 November that the commander of the Afrika Korps met with Rommel to report the situation as he saw it. He explained that he had destroyed most of the British 7th Armoured Division and the 1st South African Division. Those parts that had escaped from the battle had disappeared into the southern desert. Crüwell now requested permission to hunt them down and finish them off.

Rommel rejected this, for he had another plan. He had decided that he would use the whole of the Afrika Korps to drive eastwards towards Sidi Omar to bring some relief to the troops at the frontier. Both Panzer divisions, the Italian 132ᵃ Divisione Corazzata 'Ariete' and the 101ᵃ Divisione Motorizzate 'Trieste' would join the advance. Rommel believed that this strong mobile force loose in the rear of Eighth Army would spread panic amongst its command and throw the whole of its forces off balance. Such a bold move was sure to embarrass the British and could force a complete withdrawal, which would end in victory for his command.

Crüwell thought that this might be the wrong move at this most critical time. The commander of the Afrika Korps was sure that this was the moment to exploit the successes gained in the last few days. He now had a perfect chance to wipe out the British armour completely. With these tanks out of the way he could then concentrate on using his Panzers to eliminate the infantry. He felt that the key to the whole battle was to be found in the fighting around Sidi Rezegh and was loath to leave the British to regain their strength whilst the Afrika Korps was distracted in the east. Rommel would not be moved. He was sure that the British armour had already been written off as a cohesive force and that this was the time for bold action. The commander of Panzergruppe Afrika was confident in his own reading of the situation and, true to the image that had recently been created around him, he set his Panzers to the east with him personally leading the way standing erect in his battle wagon.

The dash to the frontier began at around 1000hrs from the area near Sidi Rezegh. It was led by Rommel and Panzer-Regiment 5. The convoys of vehicles headed south-eastwards aiming for the Trigh el Abd, intending to

A knocked-out Italian Cannone da 47/32 M35 anti-tank gun with one of its crew lying dead beside it. (IWM, E13485)

follow the track right up to the frontier. Starting later, but planning to meet up with Rommel at the border, was the 21. Panzer-Division, followed eventually by the two Italian formations. When the lead elements of this force passed the eastern end of the southern escarpment and swept out into the open desert it crashed into a string of British formations, scattering in turn the headquarters of XXX Corps, 7th Armoured Division, the Support Group and 1st South African Division. None of these vital command posts were struck head on, but the fast-moving force drove fear into the hearts of anything and anyone in its way or within range of its guns. Everywhere tanks, guns, lorries, armoured cars and carriers raced in all directions trying to get away from the mass of German transport and armour. Wherever possible, anti-tank guns and artillery peppered the flanks of the enemy columns to restore some pride in the men who were forced out of the way by the Afrika Korps, but these were only pinpricks. Rommel was immovable in his determination to reach the frontier, shrugging off any resistance and urging his force ever forwards. They reached Gasr el Abid close to the frontier at 1600hrs, having driven 100km in just six hours.

General Cunningham was at Norrie's headquarters when the German columns approached and there was a real fear that the command post might be overrun. The commander of Eighth Army made a hurried exit and reached his aircraft on the landing strip just as the first shells began falling. Fortunately he was able to escape the threat and carried on to meet with Godwin-Austen at his advance headquarters. Whilst he and the commander of XIII Corps were in conference news came in of enemy tanks and transport passing near to Gabr Saleh and later reports said that a great Panzer force was approaching the frontier. Aerial reconnaissance was ordered over the area to try to determine what was happening, but all that observers could report was that everyone, everywhere across the desert, seemed to be on the move, although it was difficult to determine friend from foe. Cunningham ordered defensive measures to be taken in all sectors and more importantly along the frontier, but nobody really knew what was happening or what Rommel was trying to do.

Fortunately, Auchinleck was still at Eighth Army's headquarters when all this confusing news came in, which was just as well for Cunningham's attitude to the German moves was one of defence. Once again the commander-in-chief saw things differently. Whilst he agreed that the 5th Indian Infantry Brigade should move to cover the railhead at Misheifa, the remainder of 4th Indian Division should stand fast and not fall back to its original positions on the frontier. The remainder of XIII Corps was to continue with operations to reach Tobruk, and XXX Corps was to carry on attacking near Sidi Rezegh, replenish its tank strength and act as flank guard for the advancing New Zealanders. The 22nd Guards Brigade was to secure the forward supply dumps in the desert from marauding enemy columns. Auchinleck did not want a defensive mentality to overtake Eighth Army; he thought all formations should look to continuing with the offensive.

Generalleutnant Crüwell reached the frontier near Gasr el Abid some hours after Rommel on 24 November. He found that Rommel had already put into progress plans for the next day, much to Crüwell's annoyance. Rommel directed that 21. Panzer-Division would cross the wire into Egypt, make a wide wheeling manoeuvre to the left and then attack westwards. The 15. Panzer-Division was to advance northwards astride the frontier. The Italian 132ª Divisione Corazzata 'Ariete' and 101ª Divisione Motorizzate 'Trieste' would attack towards Fort Capuzzo, although in the event the 101ª Divisione Motorizzate 'Trieste' did not make it to the frontier and remained in the El Adem area. British supply dumps were to be attacked wherever found and supplies, especially fuel, incorporated into German reserves.

Crüwell disliked the plan intensely. The sudden move had given horrendous administrative difficulties to the supply train and the speed of the head of the advance had caused the tail to be strung out across the desert for 80km. By the end of the day there was no sign of the 132ª Divisione Corazzata 'Ariete'. Units of the Afrika Korps were arriving piecemeal and orders were becoming confused. As Rommel met the various units he immediately dispatched the tired troops into the British lines, resulting in cases of formations receiving conflicting messages. The hard drive across the desert

A burnt-out German Panzer III destroyed during the fighting around El Duda. (IWM, E7039)

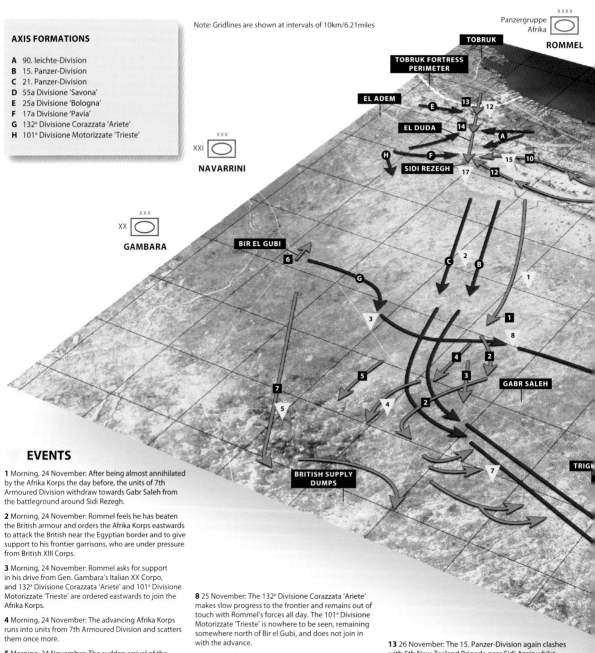

AXIS FORMATIONS

A 90. leichte-Division
B 15. Panzer-Division
C 21. Panzer-Division
D 55a Divisione 'Savona'
E 25a Divisione 'Bologna'
F 17a Divisione 'Pavia'
G 132ª Divisione Corazzata 'Ariete'
H 101ª Divisione Motorizzate 'Trieste'

Note: Gridlines are shown at intervals of 10km/6.21miles

Panzergruppe Afrika — ROMMEL

TOBRUK

TOBRUK FORTRESS PERIMETER

EL ADEM

EL DUDA

SIDI REZEGH

NAVARRINI — XXI

GAMBARA — XX

BIR EL GUBI

GABR SALEH

BRITISH SUPPLY DUMPS

TRIG

EVENTS

1 Morning, 24 November: After being almost annihilated by the Afrika Korps the day before, the units of 7th Armoured Division withdraw towards Gabr Saleh from the battleground around Sidi Rezegh.

2 Morning, 24 November: Rommel feels he has beaten the British armour and orders the Afrika Korps eastwards to attack the British near the Egyptian border and to give support to his frontier garrisons, who are under pressure from British XIII Corps.

3 Morning, 24 November: Rommel asks for support in his drive from Gen. Gambara's Italian XX Corpo, and 132ª Divisione Corazzata 'Ariete' and 101ª Divisione Motorizzate 'Trieste' are ordered eastwards to join the Afrika Korps.

4 Morning, 24 November: The advancing Afrika Korps runs into units from 7th Armoured Division and scatters them once more.

5 Morning, 24 November: The sudden arrival of the Germans in the southern desert causes alarm and the 22nd Guards Brigade is moved from Bir el Gubi to guard the southern supply dumps from attack.

6 Afternoon, 24 November: The two Panzer divisions of the Afrika Korps reach the area of the frontier. Rommel sends the 21. Panzer-Division into Egypt to drive north-east behind the scattered British forces along the frontier, whilst 15. Panzer-Division moves northwards to outflank the 2nd New Zealand and 4th Indian Divisions.

7 25 November: The Afrika Korps' extended lines of communication are attacked by 'Jock Columns' of the 7th Support Group.

8 25 November: The 132ª Divisione Corazzata 'Ariete' makes slow progress to the frontier and remains out of touch with Rommel's forces all day. The 101ª Divisione Motorizzate 'Trieste' is nowhere to be seen, remaining somewhere north of Bir el Gubi, and does not join in with the advance.

9 25 November: The 21. Panzer-Division advances northwards into Egypt looking for British supply dumps but is unsuccessful.

10 25 November: The 15. Panzer-Division advances towards Sidi Azeiz and clashes with units of the 2nd New Zealand Division but the fighting is sporadic and inconclusive.

11 25 November: The 4th Indian Division interferes with the movement of 15. Panzer-Division near Sidi Omar.

12 25 November: The 70th Division continues with its breakout battle and gradually drives forwards toward El Adem

13 26 November: The 15. Panzer-Division again clashes with 5th New Zealand Brigade near Sidi Azeiz whilst the New Zealanders were attacking towards Bardia. Breakdowns amongst the tanks and the tiredness of the crews force the division to call off the battle and it withdraws.

14 26 November: The attack northwards by the 21. Panzer-Division begins to run out of steam as supply difficulties mar the move.

15 26 November: Whilst Rommel's main forces are in the east, the 4th and 6th New Zealand Brigades make dogged advances along the escarpments near Sidi Rezegh, forging their way through to join up with the Tobruk corridor.

ROMMEL'S DASH TO THE FRONTIER

Rommel decides to make a rapid armoured advance to the Egyptian border to bring help to his hard-pressed forces holding the frontier, and at the same time cut the British lines of communication.

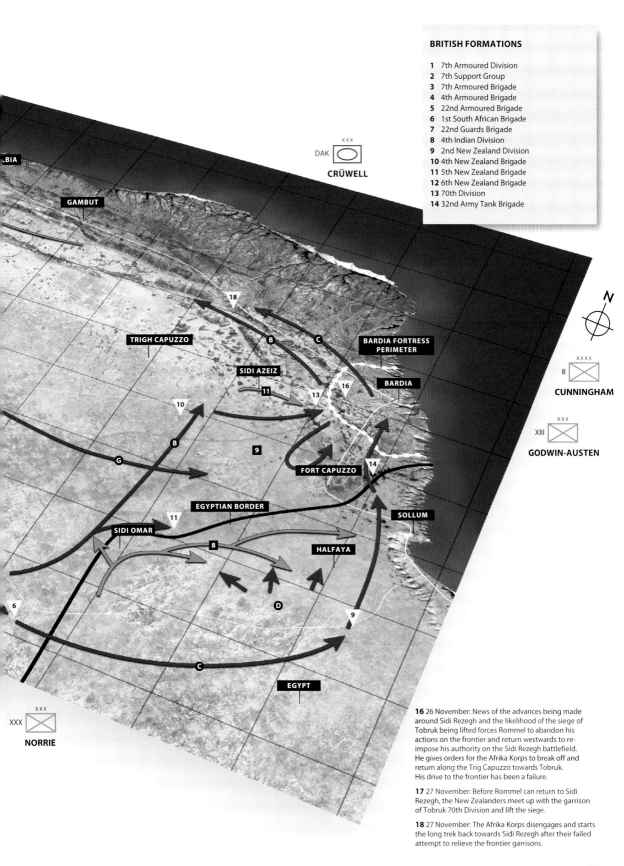

BRITISH FORMATIONS

1 7th Armoured Division
2 7th Support Group
3 7th Armoured Brigade
4 4th Armoured Brigade
5 22nd Armoured Brigade
6 1st South African Brigade
7 22nd Guards Brigade
8 4th Indian Division
9 2nd New Zealand Division
10 4th New Zealand Brigade
11 5th New Zealand Brigade
12 6th New Zealand Brigade
13 70th Division
14 32nd Army Tank Brigade

DAK ⬭ XXX
CRÜWELL

BIA

GAMBUT

TRIGH CAPUZZO

SIDI AZEIZ

BARDIA FORTRESS PERIMETER

BARDIA

FORT CAPUZZO

EGYPTIAN BORDER

SIDI OMAR

SOLLUM

HALFAYA

EGYPT

8 ⊠ XXXX
CUNNINGHAM

XIII ⊠ XXX
GODWIN-AUSTEN

XXX ⊠ XXX
NORRIE

16 26 November: News of the advances being made around Sidi Rezegh and the likelihood of the siege of Tobruk being lifted forces Rommel to abandon his actions on the frontier and return westwards to re-impose his authority on the Sidi Rezegh battlefield. He gives orders for the Afrika Korps to break off and return along the Trig Capuzzo towards Tobruk. His drive to the frontier has been a failure.

17 27 November: Before Rommel can return to Sidi Rezegh, the New Zealanders meet up with the garrison of Tobruk 70th Division and lift the siege.

18 27 November: The Afrika Korps disengages and starts the long trek back towards Sidi Rezegh after their failed attempt to relieve the frontier garrisons.

Italian prisoners awaiting interrogation after having been captured during a night-time patrol into no man's land. (IWM, 6126)

also took a heavy toll on tanks and vehicles. Panzer-Regiment 8 lost seven tanks during the long march and the 21. Panzer-Division suffered similar breakdowns in their tanks and armoured cars. Many of those vehicles that broke down remained stranded until some rescue attempt was made, for the following columns swiftly passed them by, urged on by orders from the top.

On 25 November Rommel's forces moved along the frontier trying to push the British XIII Corps, and especially the New Zealanders, northwards into the minefields at Sollum. Crüwell once again remonstrated with his commander that the troops were exhausted and that the Italians, who were to guard the left flank of these advances, had still not arrived. Rommel would have none of it and the attacks went ahead as he intended. Unfortunately for him he did not realize that only one of the New Zealand Division's brigades was ahead of him at that time. One of the others was attacking near Gambut and the third was well to the west attacking the German positions at Sidi Rezegh. Nor did he realize that the 4th Indian Division had taken Libyan Omar, Sidi Omar and Fort Capuzzo more than a day before.

When Panzer-Regiment 5 advanced northwards it was stopped near Sidi Omar by the 7th Indian Brigade. The 1st Field Regiment RA in particular put up a brave resistance to the advancing Germans. The gunners manning a line of 25-pdr guns waited until the tanks were just 750m away before opening fire with solid shot over open sights, causing great havoc amongst the advancing Panzers and Panzergrenadiers. A stiff battle ensued in which five of the British guns were knocked out and 66 of the gunners made casualties, but the resistance was strong enough to force the Panzers to withdraw. In the afternoon the German regiment tried to advance again further to the west. Again it ran into Eighth Army's artillery, this time supplemented by the fire of medium guns, and was repulsed. By the end of the day the 21. Panzer-Division had lost 18 tanks, reducing its total to just 25 runners, and it was still to the south of Sidi Omar.

The 15. Panzer-Division had advanced with its 53 Panzers to the desert between Sidi Omar and Sidi Azeiz, but its supply train was becoming so stretched that coordination was difficult. The attacks planned for that day all petered out and the whole of the division was subjected to interference from the RAF, with bombers swooping down on any enemy columns they found in the desert.

Rommel's bold plan to roll up enemy troops along the frontier was proving to be much harder to execute than he expected. His advance had brought him much closer to British air bases and all of his formations were feeling the effects of RAF missions flown from nearby airfields. The Luftwaffe could do little in return for their bases were much further away to the west. They had also lost the airfield at Gambut, which had been overrun by the New Zealand 4th Brigade. Rommel's troops were now exhausted by the previous week's fighting and were suffering the effects of the long march. Breakdowns were common, fuel and ammunition was running short, British opposition was heavier than expected and Rommel was interfering with the deployment of units down to battalion level and below. The Afrika Korps that had arrived at the frontier was more of an uncoordinated collection of fighting units rather than the efficient strike force it had been just a week earlier. And there was still no sign of the 132ª Divisione Corazzata 'Ariete'.

After having urged his formations into the attack, Rommel set off with his chief of staff and ADC (aide-de-camp) eastwards through the wire, roaming across the rear areas of the Indian Division looking for British supply dumps. Unbelievably, they motored alone in Rommel's Mammoth battle wagon, a British AEC Dorchester 4 x 4 Armoured Command Vehicle repainted in Afrika Korps colours, which had been captured earlier in the campaign. This was typical of Rommel and was a trait that exasperated the staff at his headquarters. In effect he was once again out of contact with his commanders whilst he probed forwards urging his men on. His search was fruitless and nothing to interest him was found. Rommel then ordered his driver to return back across the wire. After a few kilometres the vehicle broke down just as light was fading. None of the men on board were able to fix the fault and to everyone's consternation they were forced to remain in the open desert to await events. Soon darkness had fallen and along with it the air temperature.

Fortunately, after about an hour they were rescued by a chance coincidence that brought Crüwell's transport, another Mammoth, past that same spot of open ground. The disgruntled Rommel and his staff were taken onboard and once again Panzergruppe Afrika's commander set off for the wire, and once again ran into a problem. In the darkness the driver lost his way and could not find the gap. Try as they might, an opening could not be forced through the rolls of barbed wire and obstacles. There was nothing for it but to wait until daylight and the most senior German officer in the whole theatre now had to spend a sleepless night shivering in the cold empty desert, lost in no man's land. Through the darkness they could hear British tanks and vehicles moving about, none of the occupants of which seemed to be interested in what appeared to be one of their own senior officers' command vehicles. At first light the gap in the wire was quickly found and Rommel was able to return to Gasr el Abid.

On 26 November Rommel met with Crüwell and restated his desire to finish off the enemy at the frontier as quickly as possible. The commander of the Afrika Korps urged Rommel to reconsider his decision and return to Tobruk at once. News from Oberstleutnant Westphal, Rommel's operations officer at Panzergruppe Afrika's HQ at El Adem, indicated that there was heavy fighting around Belhamed close to the Tobruk corridor. Crüwell was convinced that the fighting in the west was the crucial part of the battlefield and was worried that whilst all his armour was at the frontier the remaining British tanks near Tobruk could operate unhindered. Once again Rommel ignored his subordinate officer and pressed for more action that day clearing the ground in front of Sollum up to Bardia.

ROMMEL LEADS THE AFRIKA KORPS' ARMOURED DRIVE TO THE EGYPTIAN BORDER THROUGH THE REAR OF EIGHTH ARMY (p.70–71)

At the height of the first battle at Sidi Rezegh Rommel was concerned that his forces away to the east at the Egyptian frontier were under a great deal of pressure from British XIII Corps. He was initially unable to offer much help to them, but after the great clash of armour on 22 and 23 November he assumed that he had broken the main strike force of British Eighth Army. He therefore decided that he could now use the whole of the Afrika Korps to drive eastwards towards Sidi Omar to bring some relief to his troops at the frontier. Both German Panzer divisions, the Italian 132ª Divisione Corazzata 'Ariete' and 101ª Divisione Motorizzate 'Trieste' would join in the advance, for Rommel believed that this strong mobile force loose in the rear of Eighth Army would spread panic amongst its command and throw the whole of its forces off balance.

The dash to the frontier began at around 1000hrs on 24 November and was led by Rommel himself accompanied by the tanks and armoured cars of Panzer-Regiment 5. The remainder of his armoured forces trailed behind at some distance. Rommel **(1)** used a British armoured command vehicle as his transport, for he liked the security of the 12mm of armoured plating afforded by its construction to ward off stray bullets. The AEC

'Dorchester' ACV **(2)** had been captured from the British earlier in the year. Three of these ACVs had fallen into German hands along with their generals, Lt. Gen. O'Connor, Lt. Gen. Neame and Maj. Gen. Gambier Parry, who were all captured near Mechili on 6 April 1941. Two of these battle wagons were used by Rommel as command vehicles in the desert which were named 'Max' and 'Morritz'. They were left with their original British camouflage markings but with the addition of large black German crosses.

Rommel's habit of leaving his headquarters to lead from the front infuriated his staff. He was often out of contact with his HQ and his formation commanders for long periods. Rommel liked to be up at the sharp end whenever he could, and his 'drive to the wire' and preoccupation with events on the frontier during the *Crusader* battle meant that the advantage he had gained at Sidi Rezegh began to slip from his grasp. Good communications systems were essential in the desert, but Rommel's desire to press on regardless often outpaced and confused those vehicles that were meant to keep up with him, such as the specialized SdKfz 251 half-track carrying signalling equipment shown shadowing his rear **(3)**.

The 15. Panzer-Division attacked towards Fort Capuzzo and ran into 5th New Zealand Brigade near Sidi Azeiz. It was clear that the New Zealanders had their main force further to the west and Crüwell realized that this formation was advancing towards Tobruk. In fact two of its brigades, the 4th and 6th New Zealand Infantry Brigades, were then in action near Belhamed only 16km from the Tobruk corridor whilst the 5th New Zealand Brigade concentrated on reducing the Italian garrison in Bardia.

Meanwhile, the 21. Panzer-Division was also attacking northwards and was finding itself up against heavy opposition near Sollum. The Italian 132[a] Divisione Corazzata 'Ariete' finally arrived near the frontier, although it never did quite reach it, and also advanced north-east towards the coast at Bardia, but did not get as far as Fort Capuzzo. Some successes were inevitably gained against the frontier forces from all this activity, but they were local and disjointed, for all these attacks were marred by a degree of confusion. Rommel and Crüwell were often giving out conflicting orders, with Rommel making impromptu changes of plan insisting that attacks go in without respite even though supplies were becoming scarce and tiredness and breakdowns were overcoming men and their vehicles. Some of the units seemed to be more concerned with foraging for fuel and food than following a barrage of conflicting orders.

All this enemy activity so close to his headquarters at Maddalena caused Cunningham more anxiety. At one point German tanks were only 45km from the main British base at Thalata. Whilst there was no panic, staff there and in fact over much of the rear area were certainly concerned. This nervousness ran through many of the people at the frontier and led to further wavering by Cunningham. Others were made of sterner stuff and were determined that the fight should go on relentlessly. Auchinleck was adamant that the offensive could still be won and felt that the commander of Eight Army was showing signs of mental and physical exhaustion, symptoms that were typical of battle fatigue. Before leaving for Cairo he left instructions for the further conduct of the battle, which included an order that was to be circulated to all fighting troops in the theatre: 'Attack and pursue', was henceforth to be the watchword of everyone in Eighth Army. Then he boarded his plane, resolved to relieve Cunningham at the head of Eighth Army.

Whilst Rommel was unsuccessfully attempting to demoralize and confuse the British by striking at their rear, activities on the west of the battlefield were turning against him, and XXX Corps was making good use of the respite given to them by the Afrika Korps' absence. The formations that had been decimated and scattered by the earlier tank battles were now regaining some cohesion, although 7th Armoured Brigade had been so badly knocked about that it was withdrawn to Egypt for a refit. Its surviving tanks were given to other units. The two remaining armoured brigades, the 4th and 22nd, repaired broken-down and damaged tanks and scoured the battlefields for others that could be brought back into service. Men rested, re-energized themselves through long hours of sleep and once again summoned new courage to enter the fray once more.

A captured 50mm German anti-tank gun is inspected by British troops. (IWM, 7049)

From 24 to 26 November Freyberg's New Zealand Division continued inching its way forwards along the Trigh Capuzzo track and the northern escarpment towards Sidi Rezegh, squeezing the German 90. leichte-Division against the guns of British 70th Division in the Tobruk corridor. This mounting pressure being brought to bear on the Axis ring around Tobruk by Eighth Army was causing alarm at Panzergruppe Afrika's HQ. The senior commander there, Obstlt. Westphal, was frantically trying to get news to Rommel but was continually frustrated by his absence from any sort of contact with his headquarters. Meanwhile the New Zealand Division fought on through bitter opposition to capture Sidi Rezegh and then Belhamed early on 26 November, and was also close to capturing El Adem. This last move was a signal for Maj. Gen. Scobie to make a major effort in his breakout battle to meet up with the New Zealanders. The siege of Tobruk seemed close to being lifted and frantic pleas for help continued to be sent to Rommel by Westphal for the return of some armoured assistance to keep the British at bay.

By this time Rommel was gradually coming to realize that events on the frontier were unlikely to get any better. Fatigue, lack of supplies, breakdowns and the strength of the British formations were all chipping away at the resolve of his fighting troops when the dire events at Tobruk were finally reported to him. It was now clear that the Afrika Korps was needed back in the Sidi Rezegh area. He reluctantly decided that he must call off his eastern venture and return his armour to the west of the battlefield. He gave instructions directly to Ravenstein to move his division towards El Duda early the next morning, whilst Neumann-Silkow's 15. Panzer-Division cleared matters up at the frontier as quickly as possible before joining 21. Panzer-Division for a combined attack on the New Zealanders. These decisions were made without the involvement of Gen.Lt Crüwell, for he was at his headquarters in the south at Gasr el Abid. He was completely out of touch with Rommel and knew nothing about these new objectives that had been given to his armour. Worse still he had no knowledge of the events at Tobruk or even the whereabouts of his two Panzer divisions.

The low ridge at Belhamed today, an area that saw much heavy fighting during the New Zealanders' attempts to meet up with the Tobruk garrison. (Western Desert Battlefield Tours)

The crew of a Stuart tank perform maintenance work to ready their mount for battle. (IWM, E7008)

Thus ended Rommel's extravagant attempt to force the British to end their offensive. It achieved very little, for Auchinleck's intervention at Eighth Army HQ and his resolve to continue the attack failed to set his forces off balance. Some minor confusion had been caused by the Axis move and there was some embarrassment at British headquarters at having enemy forces so far in their rear, but the move had not caused them to change their plans to any significant extent. Neither did the move halt events in the Tobruk area. No British supply lines were disrupted and no major supply dumps were overrun. The main outcome of the venture was that it prompted the early replacement of Eighth Army's commander.

The Germans had lost around 30 of their 100 tanks without relieving their frontier garrisons. Rommel had weakened his Panzer forces and used up vital supplies without moving the battle forwards in any way that harmed the British. Right from the start, Gen.Lt. Crüwell had tried to persuade Rommel that his first task should be to annihilate the armour of XXX Corps completely whilst he had a chance and to clear the western battlefield in order to stifle the sortie made by the Tobruk garrison. Rommel had behaved impulsively, believing too much in his own prowess as a daring commander and a proponent of mobile warfare. He was prepared to take great risks to achieve a spectacular conclusion, whereas, in this particular case, he should have perhaps acted more like a good battlefield commander and done the obvious thing to grind out a victory.

THE INFANTRY BATTLE

When Gen. Auchinleck arrived back at his Cairo headquarters on 26 November he was confronted with the problem of what to do about Lt. Gen. Cunningham. He had resolved to replace him at the head of Eighth Army, but was undecided who to replace him with. The obvious choice would have been one of his corps commanders, Norrie or Godwin-Austen, but they were in the middle of a battle and such a move would be followed by other moves all down the chain of command to fill the gaps. The change at Eighth Army needed to be made immediately even though no other senior officers capable of the task were in the theatre. Nor did Auchinleck have time for one to be flown out from England, so he looked for one from within his own headquarters and decided that his deputy chief of staff, Maj. Gen. Neil Ritchie, would have to be the man.

Neil Ritchie was much more junior than Auchinleck's corps commanders, with little experience of leading fighting troops. He had not commanded anything higher than a battalion in the field, but the circumstances at the time were critical and Eighth Army needed a new man at the top. Ritchie's elevation was meant to be only a temporary solution until the end of Operation *Crusader*. Even though he might possibly be out of his depth he would have the guidance of the commander-in-chief to ensure that all ran smoothly. Auchinleck briefed Ritchie on how he felt the offensive ought to progress and let the new commander go up to his headquarters and get on with the battle. The commander-in-chief nonetheless intended to keep a firm grip on the outcome of *Crusader* and when it looked as though the offensive was gaining the upper hand he moved to Eighth Army's headquarters at Maddalena where he remained for the next ten days.

By the early hours of 27 November the siege of Tobruk had been lifted. Major-General Scobie's 70th Division had finally met up with friendly forces. The day before it had seemed that this might not happen, for the New Zealand Division had been held up during its attack on El Duda. Scobie decided that his men should press on and take the place themselves. Aided by tanks of the 32nd Army Tank Brigade, the 1st Essex Regiment attacked out of the corridor and successfully seized the locality. During the struggle Captain J. J. B. Jackman of the Royal Northumberland Fusiliers won the Victoria Cross for bravery. Soon a New Zealand detachment from the 19th New Zealand Battalion and a squadron of the 4th RTR moved across from Belhamed to complete the junction between the two forces. Whilst Rommel was away, the one thing he had strived so hard to prevent had happened.

This moment of triumph was short lived, for the heavy fighting along the northern escarpment had taken a heavy toll on the New Zealanders and things were about to get much worse for them. Advancing from the east towards their rear were the tanks of the Afrika Korps. In the lead was 15. Panzer-Division driving along the Trigh Capuzzo, with the 21. Panzer-Division, somewhat delayed by events at the frontier, moving along the coast road, the Via Balbia. News of this advance was signalled to Norrie who decided to commit his two armoured brigades against the Germans whilst the Support Group kept the 132ª Divisione Corazzata 'Ariete' at bay on the southern side of the battlefield.

On 27 November 15. Panzer-Division was sighted on the Trigh Capuzzo just west of Gasr el Arid. Major-General Gott ordered the 22nd Armoured Brigade to head off its leading column and for 4th Armoured Brigade to

The commander of the Deutsches Afrika Korps, Gen.Lt. Ludwig Crüwell. The German corps commander was often shocked by some of the decisions made by Rommel during the *Crusader* battle. He would have preferred to have fought a more conventional action and slugged it out with the British armour, rather than keep shifting the main weight of German forces to and fro across the battlefield as Rommel did. (IWM, E12661)

Air Vice-Marshal Coningham (left), Commander Western Desert Air Force, and Lt. Gen. Neil Ritchie, the new commander of Eighth Army, in conversation with Brig. Galloway, Cunningham's chief of staff, soon after Ritchie had taken over at Eighth Army. It was Galloway's intervention with Auchinleck that prompted the command changes at the top during Operation *Crusader*. (IWM, E7000)

attack its flank. By that time the 22nd had 45 tanks operational with the 4th having 77. It was estimated that 15. Panzer-Division had about 50 Panzers. The resulting tank battle followed the form of earlier clashes with confused fighting taking place until the light began to fade, at which point the British quit the battlefield and withdrew for the night. With no tanks now in front of him, Neumann-Silkow quickly ordered the immediate replenishment of supplies and fuel to allow 15. Panzer-Division to push on in the darkness to a position on the northern escarpment from which it could continue its advance the next day, leaving the British armour at rest in the rear.

The new commander of Eighth Army had previously ordered that XXX Corps should prevent the enemy armour from penetrating the area west of Sidi Rezegh, but one Panzer division had now already slipped past Gott's tanks. Ritchie also released the 1st South African Brigade to advance northwards to meet up with the exposed New Zealanders to strengthen the grip on the northern escarpment. During 28 November the two British armoured brigades were given the task of screening the move of the South Africans across the desert. Fortunately, 21. Panzer-Division was still delayed in its move west so the only other armour to threaten this move was the 132ª Divisione Corazzata 'Ariete', and the Italians were prevented from moving westwards by the Support Group. Brigadier Pienaar was told to bring his 1st SA Brigade as quickly as possible up to the northern ridge at Point 175 to join 6th New Zealand Brigade, but by the end of the day his formation was nowhere near its objective. It had advanced only 18 of the 35km towards Point 175 when it stopped for the night.

On the ridge itself, in the triangle around Belhamed, El Duda and Sidi Rezegh, the two New Zealand Brigades endured another period of incessant shelling and minor counter-attacks, as did the men and tanks of 70th Division inside the tip of the Tobruk corridor. Few supplies had been able to get through to 4th and 6th New Zealand Brigades from the east, for the rear area was mostly under the control of German columns moving westwards after Rommel's dash to the wire. Supplies of food and ammunition were gradually running out. The headquarters of XXX Corps and the rear headquarters of the New Zealand Division both moved into the Tobruk perimeter for safety.

TOBRUK'S BELEAGUERED GARRISON MEETS UP WITH THE LEAD TROOPS OF BRITISH EIGHTH ARMY (p.78–79)

On 27 November Matilda infantry tanks from Tobruk met with units of the New Zealand Division near El Duda, bringing to an end the 240 days of siege endured by the troops defending the fortress area around the port. There to seal the historic meeting were the commander of the New Zealand 19th Battalion, Lt. Col. Hartnell **(1)**, and the commander of the 32nd Army Tank Brigade, Brig. Willison **(2)**.

On 26 November, Maj. Gen. Scobie (commander 70th Division in Tobruk) ordered Brig. Willison to capture the high ground at El Duda to the south-east, whilst the New Zealand Division's 6th Brigade advanced north-west to join it on the feature and finally raise the siege. Willison's brigade attacked with the Matilda tanks of the 4th Royal Tank Regiment **(3)** followed by the cruisers and light tanks of 1st Royal Tank Regiment with the infantry tanks of D Squadron, 7th Royal Tanks, in reserve. Infantry support was provided by the 1st Essex Regiment. After much fierce fighting they gained the ground at El Duda and then waited for the New Zealanders to help consolidate the position. However, the 6th New Zealand Brigade could make little progress northwards across the northern escarpment through the resolute German forces who held the ground, so Maj. Gen. Freyberg ordered his 4th Brigade to send its 19th

Battalion along the rear of the escarpment from the east to join up with the Tobruk breakout. It was nightfall before its commanding officer, Lt. Col. Hartnell, could get his battalion organized for the advance. It moved off in complete darkness making its 9km advance solely on compass bearings. The New Zealanders bludgeoned their way forwards, overrunning numerous enemy positions and brushing aside all opposition to reach Willison's forces early the next day. This spectacular advance finally enabled Eighth Army to join hands with the Tobruk garrison.

Brigadier Willison's 32nd Army Tank Brigade later took part in the disastrous Gazala battles the following year and was once again in Tobruk when the fortress area finally fell to Rommel's forces on 21 June 1942. Brigadier Willison himself managed to escape from the final encirclement only to be found by the Germans the following day hiding in a cave. The flag that had flown over Tobruk throughout the siege was captured by the Germans and Rommel presented it to the brigadier in recognition of the brave fight his formation had put up during the struggle to capture the fortress area. The flag remained with Willison all the time he was in captivity, but was later stolen by thieves some time after the war.

Rommel now felt he was in a position to seize back the whole of the northern escarpment and reseal the Tobruk perimeter. He ordered an assault on the Belhamed–El Duda area with 21. Panzer-Division attacking from the north and 15. Panzer-Division driving up from the south. Before this could be put into practice, the 21. Panzer-Division lost its commander when Ravenstein was captured near Point 175 by the New Zealanders. He was replaced by Generalmajor Böttcher who was in turn replaced as head of the Artillerie Gruppe by Oberst Mickl.

On 29 November the 15. Panzer-Division's attack went in as planned, but 21. Panzer-Division was slow in moving up to its start line and was not even in position by nightfall. Fighting at El Duda carried on all day and the German Panzers and their supporting Panzergrenadiers pushed the infantry of 70th Division back into the defended corridor that linked the locality to Tobruk. Later in the day a counter-attack by infantry with tank support from 11 infantry tanks of the 4th RTR won back all the ground that had been lost to the Germans.

The British armour was still to the south and was becoming involved with fighting the 132ᵃ Divisione Corazzata 'Ariete'. Ritchie ordered these two brigades to push north as soon as possible to help the New Zealanders, but both found it difficult to disengage. Some tanks and infantry from the 132ᵃ Divisione Corazzata 'Ariete' managed to sidestep the British and gain Point 175 on top of the northern escarpment and evict the New Zealanders who were holding the slight prominence. This was a blow for the 6th New Zealand Brigade, who had lost many men capturing the feature many days before. There was, however, one piece of good news, for a supply convoy from the east had driven through enemy territory to reach Freyberg's division with much-needed food and ammunition.

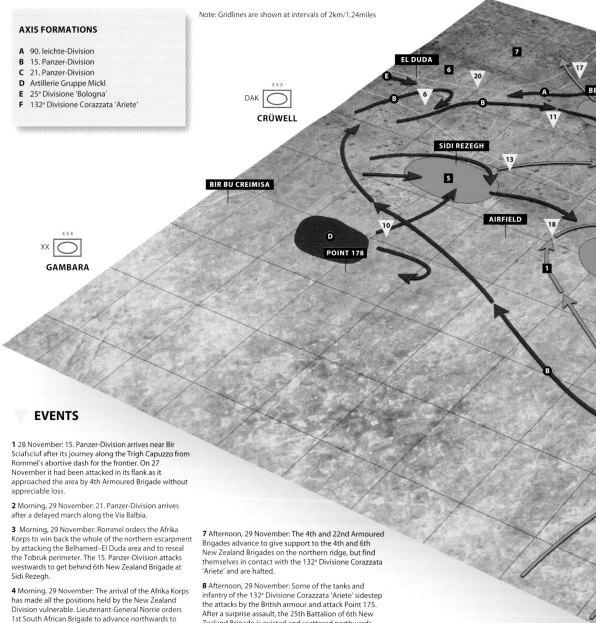

AXIS FORMATIONS

A 90. leichte-Division
B 15. Panzer-Division
C 21. Panzer-Division
D Artillerie Gruppe Mickl
E 25ª Divisione 'Bologna'
F 132ª Divisione Corazzata 'Ariete'

DAK
CRÜWELL

GAMBARA

EL DUDA

SIDI REZEGH

BIR BU CREIMISA

AIRFIELD

POINT 178

BEL

EVENTS

1 28 November: 15. Panzer-Division arrives near Bir Sciafsciuf after its journey along the Trigh Capuzzo from Rommel's abortive dash for the frontier. On 27 November it had been attacked in its flank as it approached the area by 4th Armoured Brigade without appreciable loss.

2 Morning, 29 November: 21. Panzer-Division arrives after a delayed march along the Via Balbia.

3 Morning, 29 November: Rommel orders the Afrika Korps to win back the whole of the northern escarpment by attacking the Belhamed–El Duda area and to reseal the Tobruk perimeter. The 15. Panzer-Division attacks westwards to get behind 6th New Zealand Brigade at Sidi Rezegh.

4 Morning, 29 November: The arrival of the Afrika Korps has made all the positions held by the New Zealand Division vulnerable. Lieutenant-General Norrie orders 1st South African Brigade to advance northwards to reinforce the positions around Point 175.

5 Morning, 21 November: The 21. Panzer-Division's attack is delayed when its commander, Gen.Lt. von Ravenstein, is captured by the New Zealanders. The division takes Bir Sciuearat but is unable to get into position to launch its main attack until nightfall.

6 Morning, 29 November: The 15. Panzer-Division drives westwards along the valley floor, gets behind Sidi Rezegh and moves northwards to attack 70th Division near El Duda. After making some progress, the Panzer division is counter-attacked and forced to withdraw.

7 Afternoon, 29 November: The 4th and 22nd Armoured Brigades advance to give support to the 4th and 6th New Zealand Brigades on the northern ridge, but find themselves in contact with the 132ª Divisione Corazzata 'Ariete' and are halted.

8 Afternoon, 29 November: Some of the tanks and infantry of the 132ª Divisione Corazzata 'Ariete' sidestep the attacks by the British armour and attack Point 175. After a surprise assault, the 25th Battalion of 6th New Zealand Brigade is evicted and scattered northwards.

9 Morning, 30 November: Rommel calls for an all-out attack on the New Zealanders holding the northern ridge, and the 132ª Divisione Corazzata 'Ariete' is told to advance westwards from Point 175.

10 Morning 30, November: Artillerie Gruppe Mickl attacks across the valley against the positions held by 6th New Zealand Brigade around Sidi Rezegh.

11 Morning 30, November: The 15. Panzer-Division once more attacks through the tip of the Tobruk corridor towards Belhamed.

12 Morning, 30 November: The leaderless 21. Panzer-Division attacks towards Zaafran but is held up by the 4th New Zealand Brigade.

13 Afternoon, 30 November: The 6th New Zealand Brigade resists in the face of repeated attacks until late afternoon when its two battalions holding Sidi Rezegh are forced to surrender or withdraw.

14 Evening, 30 November: Attacked and becoming increasingly isolated, the 6th New Zealand Brigade withdraws north-east to the area of Zaafran.

THE NEW ZEALAND DIVISION ON SIDI REZEGH RIDGE, 29 NOVEMBER TO 1 DECEMBER

The great tank battles of Operation *Crusader* had decimated the armoured forces of both sides. The outcome of Auchinleck's offensive now rested with the infantry, in hard-fought battles amongst the low ridges to the south-east of Tobruk.

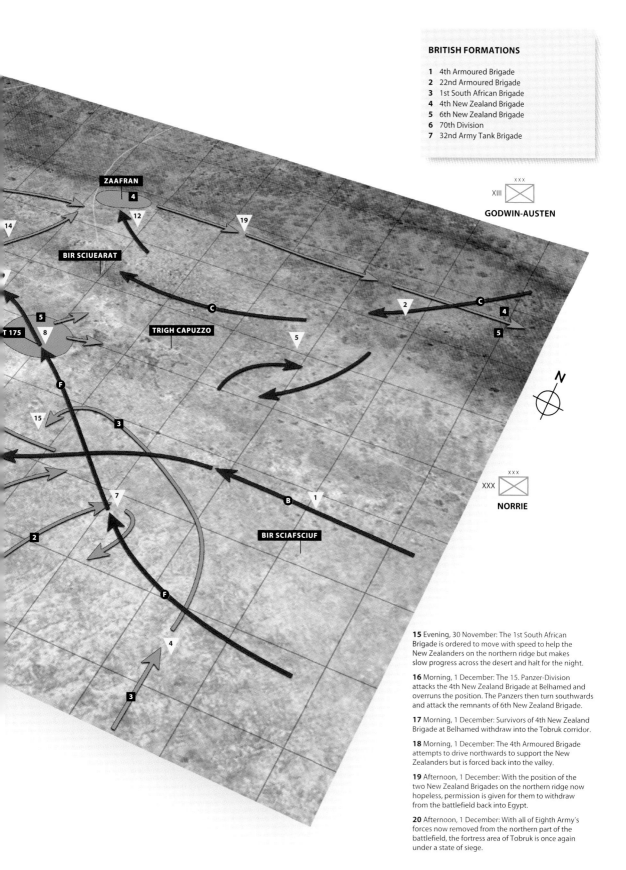

BRITISH FORMATIONS

1 4th Armoured Brigade
2 22nd Armoured Brigade
3 1st South African Brigade
4 4th New Zealand Brigade
5 6th New Zealand Brigade
6 70th Division
7 32nd Army Tank Brigade

ZAAFRAN

BIR SCIUEARAT

TRIGH CAPUZZO

T 175

BIR SCIAFSCIUF

XIII GODWIN-AUSTEN

XXX NORRIE

15 Evening, 30 November: The 1st South African Brigade is ordered to move with speed to help the New Zealanders on the northern ridge but makes slow progress across the desert and halt for the night.

16 Morning, 1 December: The 15. Panzer-Division attacks the 4th New Zealand Brigade at Belhamed and overruns the position. The Panzers then turn southwards and attack the remnants of 6th New Zealand Brigade.

17 Morning, 1 December: Survivors of 4th New Zealand Brigade at Belhamed withdraw into the Tobruk corridor.

18 Morning, 1 December: The 4th Armoured Brigade attempts to drive northwards to support the New Zealanders but is forced back into the valley.

19 Afternoon, 1 December: With the position of the two New Zealand Brigades on the northern ridge now hopeless, permission is given for them to withdraw from the battlefield back into Egypt.

20 Afternoon, 1 December: With all of Eighth Army's forces now removed from the northern part of the battlefield, the fortress area of Tobruk is once again under a state of siege.

83

The 1st South African Brigade was desperately needed to support the New Zealand Division and once again Brig. Pienaar was urged to get his formation up to Point 175. However, when news of the Italian success reached his headquarters he felt that the situation was such that he needed further clarification before moving and remained well south of this objective for the rest of the day. In the meantime, Freyberg's men were being gradually whittled away by the infantry war of attrition that was taking place on top of the ridge.

Rommel knew that he was starting to run out of time. His intelligence had informed him that the British were bringing up fresh reinforcements. He needed to remove the New Zealanders from the northern ridge and regain control of the important ground south-east of Tobruk. If he allowed the British to reinforce these positions all would be lost. His orders for 30 November were for an all-out attack on the New Zealand Division: with the 132[a] Divisione Corazzata 'Ariete' attacking from Point 175 on the eastern end of the ridge, Artillerie Gruppe Mickl capturing Sidi Rezegh, the 15. Panzer-Division advancing on Belhamed and the 90. leichte-Division moving south from its position on the Tobruk perimeter near the coast. The 21. Panzer-Division was still trying to move westwards through Zaafran, and had been since the start of the previous day's attack, but opposition there was holding it back.

It was afternoon before all the Axis attacks got under way to the accompaniment of sustained artillery fire. The 6th New Zealand Brigade held on around Sidi Rezegh with the 24th and 26th Battalions for over four hours before they were finally overrun. The tired troops from these already-depleted battalions were either killed or captured and over 600 men filed away into captivity. Major-General Freyberg was seeing his division ground down

Italian prisoners captured by the New Zealanders during the fighting to link up with the Tobruk garrison. (IWM, E6913)

The crew of a Crusader cruiser tank watch as thousands of dejected Axis troops file into captivity after Rommel's defeat. (IWM, E6742)

before his eyes and asked permission for the survivors of 6th New Zealand Brigade to be allowed to withdraw into Tobruk. Permission was refused by Godwin-Austen as the 1st South African Brigade was due to attack Point 175 and needed the New Zealanders to hold the other end of the escarpment whilst it did so.

After the delays of trying to get the 1st South African Brigade onto their objectives over the previous two days, Lt. Gen. Norrie decided that he would lead the formation into battle himself. The brigade advanced slowly on Point 175 with Norrie urging it on. The 4th Armoured Brigade provided protection for the move, but the outcome was the same as before; the advance began during the early evening, but by dawn the brigade was still 1.6km short of the feature.

On 1 December 15. Panzer-Division attacked 4th New Zealand Brigade at Belhamed. Again, after ferocious close-quarters fighting, the 20th Battalion that was holding the ground was overrun. The Panzers then turned south-east and attacked the remains of 6th New Zealand Brigade. The 4th Armoured Brigade went to help the hard-pressed New Zealanders but the Germans were already gaining the upper hand and the situation was proving hopeless. After some confusing orders and delay, both units withdrew – the New Zealanders moving northwards to join up with their 4th Brigade and the armour southwards into the valley below the escarpment.

Major-General Freyberg's units were now at the end of their physical limits. Freyberg's division had been so badly mauled that it was becoming merely a disjointed collection of individuals. The veteran general again asked for permission to withdraw the 4th and 6th Brigades from the battlefield and this time his request was granted by Lt. Gen. Norrie. The remnants of this proud division were told to fall back into Egypt for reorganzation and refit.

As they drew away from the northern escarpment and headed east, the Axis ring closed completely around the Tobruk perimeter to place the fortress area once again in a state of siege.

Rommel had cleared the vital ground to the south-east of Tobruk, apart from around El Duda, but at great cost in men and equipment. The Afrika Korps was very tired as were all the formations that had been in action with the British. Rommel admitted that the battle had become one of attrition and the outlook for his forces was grave for, unlike the British, he was not able to bring forwards fresh troops. Ritchie understood this and was determined to stay on the offensive. Auchinleck had left Eighth Army's commander to handle the battle whilst he organized the supply of new forces. With the New Zealand Division now withdrawn, its place at the front was to be taken by 4th Indian Division. The 2nd South African Division had come up from Egypt and was taking over the task of defeating the enemy positions along the frontier with 5th New Zealand Brigade under command. The 1st Armoured Division had arrived in Egypt from England and was disembarking new tanks, artillery and equipment, some of which were being sped forward to XXX Corps. Other units and formations were being transferred from Syria and Cyprus. Eighth Army was maintaining its strength whilst Rommel's command was being whittled away. The German commander now saw his chances of victory fading fast.

ROMMEL IN RETREAT

Ritchie felt that the time was approaching when Norrie's XXX Corps would be able to launch a powerful attack to drive through to Tobruk. He set 3 December as the start date and ordered all formations to be ready. Rommel's intelligence passed this news on the Panzergruppe commander who decided to use the pause to try to give some comfort to his formations on the frontier. Once again he directed the Afrika Korps eastwards along the coast road and the Trigh Capuzzo to clear away British units. Crüwell was again unhappy with any venture that faced eastwards, but nonetheless complied with the order. The attacks were hampered by bad weather and were intercepted near Bardia by Indian and New Zealand troops, and proved to be ineffective. On 4 December Rommel diverted his attention back to the west and attacked El Duda.

General Norrie had meanwhile assembled a large force near Bir el Gubi for a drive towards Tobruk. It consisted of the 11th Indian Brigade, the 22nd Guards Brigade and the 4th Armoured Brigade. The first task was to attack a German position just to the north of Bir el Gubi. This activity immediately alerted Rommel, for he feared that an assault on the rear of the Afrika Korps from this direction would be dangerous. He broke off the attack on El Duda and recalled the columns that were to the east, seeking to concentrate all his mobile forces on the southern flank to counter the British armour. He would then make his own enveloping movement around the rear of XXX Corps.

This large movement across the desert was easily spotted by the RAF and its advance was bombed all the way. On 5 and 6 December these forces clashed piecemeal with 11th Indian Brigade and then the 22nd Guards Brigade, fighting off stiff opposition during which the commander of 15. Panzer-Division, Gen.Lt. Neumann-Silkow, was mortally wounded. On the morning of 7 December Crüwell met with Rommel and told him that the British were far superior on the ground and in the air and the condition of his

Rommel's Retreat: Axis forces are pushed back hundreds of kilometres across Cyrenaica to El Agheila in Tripolitania, pursued by Eighth Army

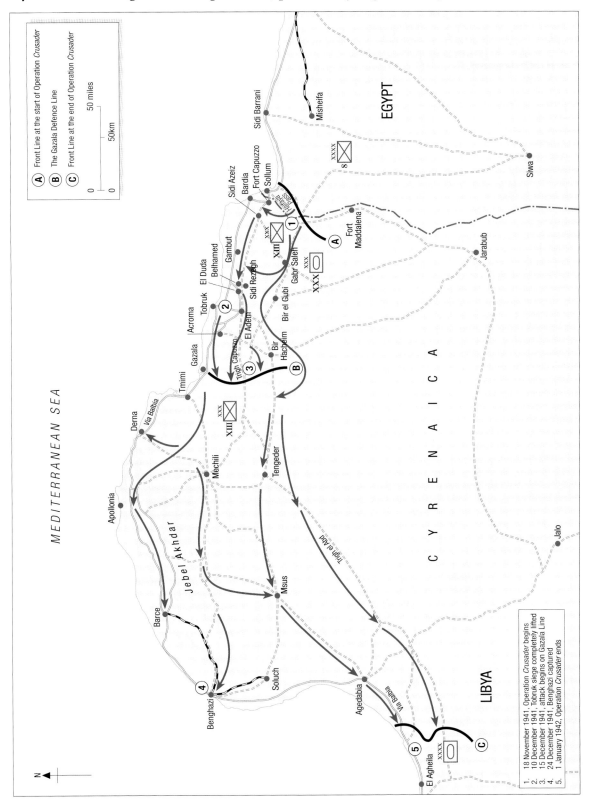

MEDITERRANEAN SEA

EGYPT

LIBYA

C Y R E N A I C A

Jebel Akhdar

Front Line at the start of Operation *Crusader*
The Gazala Defence Line
Front Line at the end of Operation *Crusader*

50 miles
50km

1. 18 November 1941, Operation *Crusader* begins
2. 10 December 1941, Tobruk siege completely lifted
3. 15 December 1941, attack begins on Gazala Line
4. 24 December 1941, Benghazi captured
5. 1 January 1942, Operation *Crusader* ends

Sidi Barrani
Misheifa
Siwa
Jarabub
Jalo
Fort Maddalena
Sollum
Halfaya Pass
Fort Capuzzo
Bardia
Sidi Azeiz
Gabr Saleh
Bir el Gubi
Gambut
Belhamed
El Duda
Sidi Rezegh
Tobruk
El Adem
Bir Hacheim
Acroma
Gazala
Trigh Capuzzo
Tmimi
Derna
Via Balbia
Apollonia
Mechili
Tengeder
Trigh el Abd
Msus
Barce
Soluch
Benghazi
Agedabia
Via Balbia
El Agheila

N

87

Towards the end of Operation *Crusader* the coast road had been cleared of the enemy. This picture was taken in mid-January two months after the start of the battle and shows an outpost overlooking the coast near Sollum. (IWM, E7689)

troops was worsening by the day. Supplies, especially fuel and ammunition, were becoming scarce. If the battle continued they faced a serious defeat. Rommel reluctantly agreed with Crüwell's opinion of the situation and gave the order for a fighting withdrawal to be made back to the prepared defensive position at Gazala, some 48km to the west. For the moment he gave up the obsession that had dominated his thoughts for the past eight months: the capture of Tobruk. The four Italian divisions now investing Tobruk were ordered to fall back and to man the Gazala line, with the Italian XX Corpo d'Armata told to protect its southern flank. The Afrika Korps were to move to a holding position in the rear. The frontier garrisons were to be left to hold out, just as Tobruk had held out against all odds.

It was some time before Eighth Army realized that Rommel was pulling back, for the German rearguard was determined that it would give up ground only at its own pace. Rommel ordered that the move was to be a fighting withdrawal and his forces were in no mood to give the British an easy passage. When XXX Corps tried to advance towards Sidi Rezegh Maj. Gen. Gott actually thought that the enemy had been reinforced, so stiff was the opposition. Norrie and Ritchie held a conference and agreed that intelligence suggested that a retreat was under way and the enemy in front of XXX Corps was reacting fiercely to cover this withdrawal. Ritchie told Norrie to keep up the pressure, but to bypass any stiff resistance where possible. Godwin-Austen was meanwhile given the task of clearing all Axis forces in the north between Tobruk and Bardia. Those of the enemy who were holding the frontier would be dealt with later. In the meantime they were to be kept bottled up in their fortified positions.

On 8 December Eighth Army was again on the move. The 23rd Brigade from 70th Division broke out of its corridor and advanced to El Adem. To the south the 7th Armoured Division drove north-west into the desert below Tobruk to a track junction which was later to be dubbed 'Knightsbridge' in future battles. The 4th Indian Division began steps to link together XIII and XXX Corps' fronts. These advances were slow affairs as Rommel's forces gradually pulled back. The now-tired British troops probed the enemy, snapping at their heels and occasionally catching unwary units that were too slow to escape. Help was available from the Desert Air Force to harass the Axis moves, for the RAF now had air bases much closer to the action as the landing strips near Gambut and around Tobruk were captured. The two sides were drawing apart and the lines of enemy vehicles on the tracks leading westwards could be easily identified and strafed by pilots without fear of hitting their own side. One notable casualty of these fighter sweeps was the commander of the 90. leichte-Division, Gen.Maj. Max Sümmermann, who was killed during the retreat.

By 10 December the Italian 27ᵃ Divisione 'Brescia' and 102ᵃ Divisione 'Trento' had withdrawn from the perimeter around the western side of Tobruk and the siege that had been in place since 11 April was well and truly lifted. Operation *Crusader* was not yet over for there was still more fighting to be done before Axis forces were totally removed from Cyrenaica, but Tobruk had been freed, Rommel was in retreat and spirits in the British camp were exceedingly high.

British 25-pdr guns of a field artillery battery bombard the enemy retreat. The openness of the desert made these gun positions and their crews vulnerable to enemy counter-battery fire. (IWM, E7161)

AFTERMATH

On 9 December both sides made command changes. The desert war was still under the overall control of the Italians and the chain of command above Rommel still passed up through Commander-in-Chief North Africa, Generale d'Armata Bastico to the *commando supremo*, Maresciallo Ugo Cavallero in Rome, but Rommel was now made the field commander of all Axis forces in the theatre, which allowed him to commit Italian forces where and how he wished on the battlefield.

Changes on the British side amounted to a reorganzation of the forces in the field. Godwin-Austen's XIII Corps would now control operations against the retreating enemy. Ritchie had decided that only one corps commander should be able to control all troops west of Tobruk. These forces would be maintained through the supply base at Tobruk and as XIII Corps was already there it made sense to give the task of pursuing Rommel to Godwin-Austen. Norrie felt that such mobile operations should be given to his XXX Corps as it was more suitable for the task, but Auchinleck intended to withdraw Norrie's corps back to Egypt as GHQ reserve. Ritchie therefore ordered the one still-active armoured brigade left in XXX Corps, 7th Armoured Division's 4th Armoured Brigade, to be transferred to XIII Corps. The 22nd Guards Brigade was placed under Ritchie's direct command and given the task of driving across the southern desert to capture the port of Benghazi and stop the enemy escaping into Tripolitania.

German prisoners of war marching into captivity at the end of the battle. Over 10,000 German and almost 20,000 Italians were captured during the two-month-long operation. (IWM, E6745)

By 13 December the enemy had withdrawn behind the Gazala position and Eighth Army had closed up to the defensive line that stretched down from Gazala on the coast to the Alem Hamza ridge and then into the barren southern desert where it petered out. Godwin-Austen planned to attack the position with the 5th New Zealand Brigade, the Polish 1st Carpathian Brigade from Tobruk, the 4th Indian Division and the 7th Support Group. The 4th Armoured Brigade was to make a wide sweeping movement in the desert south of the line's right flank with its 90 tanks to get at the remaining 50 or so Panzers that the Afrika Korps had in the rear. This was the move that Rommel feared most and he explained to Bastico that if the British successfully attempted such an outflanking manoeuvre he would have no option but to withdraw right back across Cyrenaica into Tripolitania. The Italian commander tried to persuade him that the loss of Cyrenaica and the port of Benghazi would cause great embarrassment back in Rome, but Rommel insisted that it was the only sane military option left to him.

The British attack began on 15 December with the infantry tying up enemy troops in the Gazala line in a struggle where some gains were made against the Italians, but losses were suffered when tackling the Germans, although nine of Panzer-Regiment 8's 23 tanks were destroyed in the action. With the enemy's main forces tied down by these frontal attacks, Godwin-Austen now released 4th Armoured Brigade at their rear.

The brigade had to drive over 115km across the desert before it could swing northwards, and this advance was slowed by winter rains and soft sand making movement difficult. By the next day it was still not in a position to launch a decisive action. Godwin-Austen urged the brigade on, but refuelling difficulties disorganized the attack and the enemy started slipping away. Rommel had seen what was happening and ordered a general withdrawal to positions at Agedabia near the border with Tripolitania.

From this point on the last days of Operation *Crusader* became a chase, with Eighth Army trying to outflank the enemy to bring his disorganized forces to battle and Rommel determined to evade a stand-up fight in order to bring as many of his formations back to Agedabia as he could. The 4th Indian Division followed the enemy around the long coast road whilst the 7th Support Group shadowed the moves along roads further inland. Benghazi was taken on 23 December. The 7th Armoured Division took a shorter route across the desert via Mechili through Msus down to Beda Fomm. Rommel intended to hold off the mobile British columns coming across the desert at Agedabia to allow Italian formations near the to coast to escape to the south. By 27 December the British were closing around the enemy at Agedabia and Crüwell asked Rommel for permission to attack the British armour. Permission was granted and on 28 December the Afrika Korps turned on the British near Mersa Brega. The 90 tanks of the 22nd Armoured Brigade were attacked by about 60 tanks from the two Panzer divisions. The British were driven back in a stiff action that cost them 37 tanks for the loss of just seven Panzers. Rommel knew that he would have to withdraw even further, back to the point where he started his spectacular advance eastwards some months before at El Agheila, but told Crüwell to keep fighting to allow the infantry to rest and refit. The Afrika Korps attacked again on 30 December and knocked out 23 more British tanks. It was some comfort to the dispirited German forces, but it was only a slight reprise for Rommel gave orders on 1 January 1942 for a further withdrawal into the positions at El Agheila. Operation *Crusader* was now over. Both sides had fought to the end of their

The victors of Operation *Crusader* at Eighth Army Headquarters. From left to right: Gen. Auchinleck; Air Vice-Marshal Coningham, Commander of the Western Desert Air Force; Lt. Gen. Neil Ritchie, Commander Eighth Army; Brig. Galloway, Ritchie's chief of staff and Captain Grantham, Royal Navy Liaison Officer. (IWM, E6998)

General der Panzertruppe Erwin Rommel, Commander Panzergruppe Afrika. Before the *Crusader* battle he had built a sound reputation as an armoured commander. Immediately after the British operation he was shown to be capable of being defeated in the desert, provided he was opposed by strong forces commanded by resolute and skilful commanders. (IWM, HU 5623)

ability and now paused to regain their strength. There was to be no more advance and no more retreat, at least not for a while.

Auchinleck had won a great victory with Operation *Crusader*. Rommel and his forces had been forced into full retreat and made to give up the whole of Cyrenaica. The victory belonged to Auchinleck himself, whose reading of the battle was masterful as was his determination to ignore Rommel's manoeuvring and concentrate on grinding down the opposition. Old-fashioned generalship had, in this instance, got the better of flamboyant mobile operations.

The casualty figures for the campaign up to the first half of January reveal the intensity of the fighting. The British had lost 2,900 men killed, 7,300 wounded and 7,500 missing – a total of 17,700, which amounted to 15 per cent of its total force. The Germans lost 1,100 killed, 3,400 wounded and 10,100 missing – a total of 14,600 men. The Italians lost 1,200 killed, 2,700 wounded and 19,800 missing, which amounted to a total casualties figure for all Axis forces of 38,300 men, or 32 per cent of their total force. Losses of equipment were equally severe. The British had around 600 cruiser tanks destroyed through battle damage and breakdowns along with around 200 infantry tanks. Axis armoured losses were thought to be 220 German and 120 Italian tanks.

As the two sides faced each other in early January near El Agheila, circumstances began to change. Panzergruppe Afrika had been chased out of Cyrenaica by a stronger force, but that strength had by now all but disappeared. Eighth Army was now worn out by almost two months of fighting. Its supply lines stretched back for hundreds of kilometres across the desert and its armoured strike force had been blunted by battle and breakdowns. It had won the *Crusader* battle but had not destroyed the enemy, for Rommel still had his command structure intact. His army was now closer to their main port of Tripoli with shortened supply lines, and the lull in the fighting was allowing it to build up its strength once again.

Rommel's logistics situation now quickly improved as supplies gradually made their way across the Mediterranean. On 5 January an Italian convoy arrived in North Africa bringing a range of new German equipment, which included 54 new tanks, 20 armoured cars and a good supply of anti-aircraft and artillery guns. Fuel and ammunition was also shipped in together with infantry reinforcements. Rommel, still smarting from the blow struck by the British, began contemplating going back on the offensive. Ritchie was of the opinion it would take the German commander months to be ready to do so, but on 21 January the Panzers once again began to roll eastwards. The move caught the weak British forces near El Agheila by surprise and they fell back. The more Rommel pushed forwards the more ground he regained. Eighth Army's outposts were set into full retreat and then the main body of the force also fell back. The retreat took them all the way back to Gazala and then finally, after many battles and much more fighting, to El Alamein in Egypt.

THE BATTLEFIELD TODAY

Operation *Crusader* was fought on the flat, sandy floor of an inhospitable desert: a barren void of wasteland with few prominences. The sparse tracks that edged their way across that unremarkable terrain often became the only recognizable features to be seen. Compasses and map references were the means by which formations moved over the desert, their men navigating their way across the sandy wilderness almost like guiding ships at sea. It is therefore not surprising that a visitor to the battlefields over which Operation *Crusader* was fought is confronted by vast monotonous wastes, searing heat and a landscape devoid of any identifiable landmarks.

This is not, however, the whole truth, for some actions were fought for the capture or defence of particular locations which even in the desert have left some identifying characteristics. For example, the old Sidi Rezegh airfield landing light is still there, and so is the former HQ building and the blockhouse captured by the New Zealanders to the south-east of Sidi Rezegh. The airfield 2km from the mosque is still protected by a minefield. It is possible, if accompanied by knowledgeable guides, to find and visit many of the places mentioned in the text. It is, however, well to remember that the remoteness of the desert has meant that dangers remain undisturbed from the time of the conflict. Unexploded ordnance, especially mines, can be encountered everywhere off the main tracks and routes and still poses a great hazard to the unwary.

Libya has only recently become more accessible to outside visitors from the west and is not yet geared up for great numbers of tourists. For this reason, and considering the difficulties raised above, it is probably best that any individual wishing to visit the *Crusader* battlefield today should travel with an established battlefield tour operator. These people will organize the visit in such a way that the most interesting locations can be visited safely. Such companies and their tours can be found listed on various Internet websites.

The Commonwealth War Graves Commission's cemetery at 'Knightsbridge'. The cemetery is situated to the south of Acroma near the location of much heavy fighting during the later battles along the Gazala line. (Western Desert Battlefield Tours)

FURTHER READING AND BIBLIOGRAPHY

One of the most important books covering Operation *Crusader* is the *British Official History of the Mediterranean and Middle East Volume III*. This gives a general view of the factual details of the offensive and its outcome. To add more individual detail and colour to the narrative I recommend Barrie Pitt's *Auchinleck's Command* from his trilogy about the war in the desert: *The Crucible of War*. The *Rommel Papers* is always a good start to find out the intimate thoughts of the German commander and George Forty's the *Armies of Rommel* fills in many details regarding the Axis forces. Thought-provoking is Michael Carver's *Dilemmas of the Desert War*, which covers the command decisions made during the battle.

Anon, *The Tiger Kills* (HMSO: London, 1944)

Braddock, D. W., *The Campaigns in Egypt and Libya 1940–1942* (Gale and Polden: Aldershot, 1964)

Carver, Michael, *Dilemmas of the Desert War: The Libyan Campaign 1940–1942* (Batsford: London, 1986)

Delaney, John, *Fighting the Desert Fox* (Arms and Armour: London, 1998)

Forty, George, *The Armies of Rommel* (Arms and Armour: London, 1997)

Fraser, David, *Knight's Cross: The Life of Field Marshal Erwin Rommel* (Harper Collins: London, 1993)

Irving, David, *The Trail of the Fox: The Life of Field Marshal Erwin Rommel* (Weidenfeld & Nicholson: London, 1977)

Joslen, Lt. Col. H. F., *Orders of Battle: Second World War 1939–1945* (HMSO: London, 1960)

Liddell Hart, Capt. B. H. (ed), *The Rommel Papers* (Collins: London, 1953)

Liddell Hart, Capt. B. H., *The Tanks: The History of the Royal Tank Regiment, Volume Two* (Cassell: London, 1959)

Pitt, Barrie, *The Crucible of War: Auchinleck's Command* (Cassell: London, 2001)

Playfair, Maj. Gen. S. O., *The Mediterranean and Middle East, Volume III* (HMSO: London, 1960)

Verney, Maj. Gen G. L., *The Desert Rats: The History of the 7th Armoured Division* (Hutchinson: London, 1954)

INDEX

Figures in **bold** refer to illustrations